"Armed with a truly remarkable capacity for humor, melancholy, and honesty, Bruce Coffin pursues a dialogue with long-dead relatives and neighbors who nonetheless still live and speak in his heart. This moving and beautifully written book deserves a wide audience."

—John Elder, author of *Reading the Mountains of Home.*

Among Familiar Shadows

"Utterly free of jargon and sentimentality, *Among Familiar Shadows* is a deep meditation of place and family, of personality traits and the circumstances by which they are amplified, grappled with, and survived. But beyond this is a study of how family peculiarities lurk and dimple through generations, past, present and to come. Bruce Coffin's great gift is his eloquent understanding of humanity's standing within the flow of time, ever changing, ever abiding."

—Jeffrey Lent, author of the national bestseller *In the Fall* and other critically acclaimed novels.

"Like Thoreau, another New Englander before him, Bruce Coffin is aware that if we only open our eyes and truly look. we can possess in imagination all that we see. And much!... *Among Familiar Shadows* is a powerfi testament to the fact that, even long after the ancestors remain alive to us in the places we sha and in our own habits of being."

—Chris Forhan, poet and author of *My Fe*

"*Among Familiar Shadows* is a beautifully rendered inspection of life. Bruce Coffin has recreated his family history, long gone but not very far away. With gorgeous prose and granular detail, his recollections are both remarkable and relatable. What pure delight in story telling!"

> —Marcia Butler, author of *The Skin Above My Knee*, a memoir, and *Pickle's Progress*, a novel.

"In this book Coffin brings his forebears—their sorrows, their delights, the cataclysmic events which changed their lives for ever—to vivid articulate life. Coffin sees and feels with such intensity that I found myself envying his dead their insightful witness, while also greedily lapping up the book as a manual for how to engage more deeply with others and be more fully alive."

> —Susan Elderkin, author of *Sunrise Over Chocolate Mountains* and *The Voices*.

"Woodstock, Vermont is Bruce Coffin's ancestral home, his source, his touchstone and inspiration. He mines it the way Faulkner mined his section of the country, except that Coffin's characters are real people. I will reread this new book, *Among Familiar Shadows* the way I reread his first book, delighting in Coffin's stories, in his prodigious and detailed memory, in his way with language, in the imagery, clear and even poetic, that appears time and again in his writing."

> —Chuck Gundersen, author of *You Never Can Tell*.

"I am fascinated by Coffin's ability and determination to recall all the details of Woodstock, its people and the surrounding land. Pure genius. I am reminded of Thornton Wilder's *Our Town*, the novels of Henry James, the precision of Proust, and the songs of Thoreau. But Coffin's talent and love are all his own. This is a New England elegy that will endure."

> —Bill Henderson, Editor, Pushcart Prize.

Also by Bruce Coffin:

The Long Light of Those Days

Among Familiar Shadows

MEMORIES AND REFLECTIONS

Bruce Coffin

Swallow Tail Press

Among Familiar Shadows

Copyright © 2020 by Bruce Coffin

Published by Swallow Tail Press
Philadelphia, PA, USA
www.swallowtailpress.com

Cover design by Matt Wood.
Interior design by Bruce Hartman.

Cover photographs courtesy of the Coffin family and the Woodstock History Center

Author photo by Peter Lennox-King

"In a Manner of Speaking" previously appeared in *Vermont Magazine.*

ISBN: 978-0-9997564-5-4

For Maria, Lizzie and Jonathan

Memories and Reflections

Blackberrying

Nature 'talks' to man in the sense that perception is experienced as meaning. — KATHLEEN RAINE

B ack in the 1980s, when my wife, Maria, and I and our young children spent some time each summer in Vermont with my mother and father, I renewed an old and deep acquaintance with the land of my forebears. Every morning I'd arise early and go up to South Pomfret to join the boys who gathered around the butcher-block table in the back of the Teago General Store for their morning coffee. My cousin Jim Jillson, who, like myself, was in his 40s then, presided over those meetings, and every year he would mention, sometime in late July, that the blackberries had already begun to ripen and that it looked as though it was going to be a good year for them. They were all mine, he'd proclaim; he was not at all interested in them. At that moment, whatever else I had planned for the next two weeks or so, I'd know I had no choice. I'd finish my coffee and go back to the house, and I would find the old berry pails in the bottom cupboard of the pantry and flatten a paper towel in the bottom of each of them. Then I'd put on an old pair of khakis and an old long-sleeved work-shirt, pack a couple of sandwiches in a bag, fill a big jar with ice water and head for the hills, hoping Jim was right.

Why some years produce a greater crop of blackberries than others is something of a mystery. Various explanations abound, some of them more like folklore than botanical fact: my uncle used to tell me simply, "too much heat's not good for 'em." The narrator in Forrest Carter's *The Education of Little Tree* claims that after "April gets its warmest," the temperature needs to drop so that "it stays cold for four or five days. This is to make the blackberries bloom and is called 'blackberry winter.' The blackberries will not bloom without it." There may some truth to this notion, though I have never remembered to keep my eye on the thermometer in April to test it out. A forester friend of mine is not persuaded and tells me it's really more a matter of the right amount of sunshine and rain during pollination, adding that the biggest and best crop of blackberries he has ever seen was in Eastport, Maine in foggy and damp conditions. I suspect it is really a combination of factors, but whatever the truth may be, I don't recall a year when they failed to appear somewhere, whether in greater or lesser abundance, and I trusted Jim, whose world was the Pomfret hills, to tell me where he had spotted them, and, in his own peculiar way, to assure me he wanted nothing to do with them.

Blackberries, for me, meant South Pomfret. My mother and her five brothers and sisters were born on a farm there on what is now Bartlett Brook Road, and they lived there until the Depression, when they were forced to sell and move back to a house they owned in the village. For all of the family, the loss of the farm was deeply felt, though they were somewhat compensated by an arrangement made with the new owners, the Gregg family from Cambridge, Massachusetts, whereby my grandfather would serve as their caretaker and have use of the house (which served the Greggs as a vacation home) for family picnics and reunions. My grandfather, Hal Jillson, was to me a kind of Rip van Winkle character. He had a great love of the Pomfret hills dating back to the 1880s and 90s when, as a child, he had walked them with his father and grandfather, once even spending part of a winter in a cabin they had constructed when they were logging a large patch of forest, and he was happiest when he was wandering in search of ginseng or wild apples or raspberries and blackberries, or just walking by himself or with some of his children or grandchildren. He had a voice that crackled with the laughter in it, and he often sang as he walked—"Camptown Races," "Tenting Tonight," "Turkey in the Straw," "Tramp, Tramp, Tramp"—with me and Jimmy and our cousin Abe and my brother in our high-top black sneakers and dungarees and summer crew cuts falling into step behind him. We might sing along, but it was more fun just to listen, for he was apt to change the lyrics to suit his love of foolishness, as in "Oh, dear what can the matter be, two old maids tied to an apple tree." I could remember large family outings when he and my mother and grandmother and aunts and my brother and sister and our cousins would all be out there in midsummer picking raspberries all morning. Then someone would give a shout or a whistle from the chosen shady spot under a big maple tree to bring us all together for a picnic lunch of sandwiches and my grandmother's watermelon pickles and cupcakes with her special raspberry frosting, and after a short nap, we'd disperse and be back at it again, with us children, our berry pails hanging off our belts nearly to our knees, eating most of what we picked. Thus was this entire area sanctified by memory for three generations, and I never even considered choosing some other location for my labors.

The farm, which has consisted of the house only since the barn was struck by lightning and burned to the ground in 1969, is still in the Gregg family and looks much as it did back in my childhood. My usual routine was to drive past it and park along the side of the dirt road near the old Webster place. From there I'd pick my way up the slope that had been cleared some years before, all the way to the top. Then, after working the most thickly growing and cruelest patch, I'd branch out and roam across the hilltops wherever the blackberry bushes led me. As anyone who has picked blackberries knows, it can be a pretty nasty and exacting business. Blackberry thorns are longer and sharper than raspberry thorns, and it is impossible to reach all the berries you want without getting your hands pretty well raked. Long sleeves buttoned at the cuff are essential, even on hot days when the impulse would otherwise be to switch to short sleeves or a t-shirt or no shirt at all. It is one thing to pick around the periphery and quite another to squirm your way into the middle where the real treasure often lies, and it is necessary to handle the bushes continually, both to gain entrance and to lift the branches to discover those berries that are the largest and ripest, growing down low and out of sight in the shade. Berry picking is a job for two hands, as I learned years ago, though I have been with one-handed pickers, neophytes who held the pail with one hand and picked with the other until I showed them how to attach the pails to their belt or suspend them from a piece of rope hanging around the neck. In that way you can pick faster, using both hands, and you can stay in one place for as long as necessary without going through the painful process of exiting for a fresh pail and then having to reenter the thicket.

Since our blackberries do not grow on hedges as they do in Great Britain and Ireland, where they may easily be harvested by people simply walking along the lanes and roads, blackberrying in America, especially among the tallest and most thickly growing bushes, is not easily carried out in the company of other people. As children, picking in the same patch with others in the family and often dwarfed by the berry bushes, we seemed to spend as much time calling out and looking for each other as we spent looking for berries. During the times when my mother would decide to go up into the hills for a few hours with me, we'd start out picking together and talking, but would eventually wander off until we were quickly out of each other's sight. Then, after a time, one would become mindful of the other and call out, usually to be surprised by the proximity or distance of the answer. Oddly enough, though blackberry picking was my enterprise then and she was in the role of my assistant, it always seemed that we had simply turned back the clock and I was tagging along, as it were. More often than not, Mother would cover more ground than I, for she was more selective in her picking. Rather than staying in one place and all but stripping the bushes, she would move around and select only the choicest fruits. And yet, in the final tally, she would somehow have picked as many, and usually more, than I.

Whatever her secret was, I never learned it. Blackberries would become a true social occasion and a family enterprise not during our work out in the hills but back at home in the late afternoon or early evening when it was time to pick them over. Then the card tables would come out onto the porch, and while the light of the long days lasted, we'd spread the berries out on paper towels and place the best ones in pint and quart baskets to be given away or sold to specified customers or taken to stores and farmers' markets. Time was of the essence here if the berries were to be delivered fresh (I learned the hard way not to let them sit over night, especially in very warm weather, until they took on what Seamus Heaney calls "a fur, a rat grey fungus" and had to be thrown away), so we'd all take part; my mother and I would be joined by my father and my wife and even our children, who would participate in some small way, though their favorite part of it all was going with me to sell the berries to Gillingham's Store. We'd wait there long enough to see our baskets, recognizable always by the way they were heaped up with berries, put out with all the other pro-duce, and, if we were lucky, we'd see them selected by a customer and purchased at the cash register.

But however much blackberries, once gathered, may bring people together, it is best to pick them by oneself, as I usually did. Were I once again to set out into those hills with my berry pails, I'd leave home unencumbered by wrist watch and cell phone, those devices which prevent that necessary, complete engagement of the senses with blackberries, in varying stages of ripeness, showing themselves in their differing shape and texture so as to indicate the firmness or delicacy of touch required to disengage each one from its stem. They narrow the field of vision among the bushes with their leaves and thorns and entanglements until a true absorption in the task both focuses the mind and leads it where it will. For there is something mysterious about natural facts: when they claim us completely, it is as though to remind us we can never see all around them, and the side facing away from us, as it were, is our invitation to dream. While I was thus attached to the earth and riveted to blackberries and my hands were busy picking, my inner wanderings would carry me out and away until, time out of mind, I'd be lost in a way possible only in places as long and deeply familiar as the Pomfret hills. It would take the buzzing of a honeybee on a nearby wild rose bush or the late summer dirge of the crickets, or the cawing of a crow passing over on his way to distant places to bring me back, and I'd look up, disoriented, at the world immediately before me—the sun having traveled west, the old hills there under a different slant of light, the wind moving a slowly passing, high white cloud and riffling the top leaves of a nearby poplar—all of it transfigured and strangely attentive. As though my industry, carried out while I was far away, had been a kind of waiting for the moment when the landscape becomes something that knows we are there, and we are awakened, found by something ancestral. In that instant, I have heard myself answer, "I am here"—words uttered reflexively, spoken in tongues as it were, to be understood or not only after they have sounded their strange acknowledgement of both agency and surrender, as though to some god in passing. Our best views of nature are always peripheral ones; searched for, it will not reveal itself as it does to those who are moving about, actively engaged in some necessary journey or task. Such brief glimpses as I was afforded each year I received like revelations, and I longed for their perpetuation—as the poet Robert Hass yearns to possess the fullness of a richly sensuous moment by his simple, almost ritual, act of extended naming, "saying blackberry, blackberry, blackberry." Annually, these moments became my true harvest, though, in Rilke's words, my "precise purpose . . . I would almost like to say . . . my obvious excuse" was berry picking, and I came out with pails and pails of shining fruit to show for my time and efforts, with fingers stained purple for weeks, and a vision of nothing but blackberries every time I closed my eyes on the way to sleep. My other, less material garnerings I kept to myself.

I was always happy that the first person I met when I had worked my solitary way down to the car in the late afternoon or early evening was my cousin Jim, coming back from stacking or splitting wood in his woodlot. Though he was no berry picker, he was curious enough about my day's accomplishments to pull his pickup truck over and get out for a look at what I'd gathered and to spend a few minutes shooting the breeze. Why, he wouldn't ever waste any time at all picking any more than was necessary for a pie or maybe a shortcake, and even then he wouldn't go very far to find them! What was I going to do with them all, anyway? It was an exchange we had every year at least once. I learned early enough not to tell him I was in it for the pure enjoyment of picking: "Enjoyment? Then you must be some kind of masochist; your shirt's all ripped, and your hands are all cut and scratched!" And my practical answers—profit from sales, satisfaction at giving some away, the taste of my mother's blackberry pies—were never quite enough for him. So sometimes I just said that in fact it was all just for the sake of how good that cold quart of Budweiser from Teago Store was going to taste at the end of my long day's work; he could accept that, though with the assertion that he himself didn't need any kind of strenuous work to achieve the same thing. We left it at that. In truth, I was no more evasive with him than I was, by necessity, with myself. I'm sure he knew I wasn't giving him the whole truth, or as much of it as I was able to understand. And it occurs to me now that he may have suspected I was shying away from speaking about something which he too had often glimpsed in the intervals of his labors in the fields and woods. At any rate, in spite of his skepticism, or posture of skepticism if that's what it was, he would always leave the blackberry bushes growing at the edge of the pastures it was his job to mow until the season had passed or I had told him I was finished with them.

Berry pickers are by nature trespassers, and my grandfather's trespassing was my inheritance. It used to be that when I was discovered rambling along with my berry pails on someone's land in South Pomfret, I could identify myself as a Jillson on my mother's side and mention my grandfather by name, and that would be enough to let me carry on for as long as I might wish. But now that more and more of the land has been bought up by strangers from out of state, it is not so easy, as I discovered in 1987 when I was accosted by two flatlanders, a man and his wife, who had seen my car parked along the side of the road next to their property and taken the trouble to track me down in their Land Rover. When they introduced themselves as the owners of the land and said they were wondering what I was doing on it, I identified myself by name and pointed at the pails hanging off my belt. To his announcement that it was not my property, I answered that I had been walking these hills long before he ever knew they existed with my grandfather, who in his time had walked it with . . . (until I must have sounded like the Old Testament) and so I liked to think the land belonged to me in a way that had nothing to do with title and deed and legal ownership. Taken aback by my boldness, he was supported by his wife, who claimed that someone else—meaning, of course, the two of them—might like to have some berries to pick for themselves, an absurd objection, as I let her know by a sweep of the arm and a reminder that I could not possibly begin to pick all the berries growing there even if I were out there 24/7 throughout the entire season. It ended in a sort of stalemate: I went on picking, and they drove off, and thereafter I simply parked somewhere else and worked my way back onto their land and never encountered either one of them again with or without berry pails.

What right does anyone have to lay solitary claim to a crop he has lost no sweat in cultivating? Had I been better prepared for their sudden arrival, I would have simply spoken the words that had come to be a credo in my family since we first heard them from my Grandmother Coffin. As she told the story, a somewhat simple woman she had known, or heard about from her parents, was picking berries on land that belonged to someone else and was caught red-handed and berated by the owner. Though no doubt intimidated, if not somewhat frightened, she stood her ground as best she could and heard him out, and then answered him quietly: "Berries is for all folks," she said, and she went right on picking.

The great patches where I labored, mostly alone and undetected, for so many summers are now grown in with brush and trees, and my cousin Jim has been gone for almost twenty years. The land in that region has changed hands several times as it has all over Vermont; more and more of the smaller farms which could no longer compete with the giant conglomerates of agribusiness have been gentrified to rustic vacation or retirement properties, and the old South Pomfret families to whom they once belonged, in some cases for many generations, have long since disappeared until even their names—Jillson, Perry, Badger, Luce, Heselton, Bartlett, Webster—which the wanderer might invoke to identify and authenticate himself by association if called upon to do so, are recognized only by a dwindling number of natives. Wild blackberries outlast us all. When the Irish playwright John Synge sought an analogy for the immortality of the greatest works of art, he said they "can no more go out of fashion than the blackberries on the hedges." Though they may no longer be growing where we once found them, they will miraculously arrive on schedule every year in their eternal return somewhere on land that has been recently cleared or at the edge of a meadow. Like divine grace, blackberries are freely given, and while they flourish under the late summer sun, they are ours for the taking.

In a Manner of Speaking

Though a sixth generation Vermonter herself, my mother was often puzzled and amused by what she regarded as the northern Yankee's disinclination to answer in the direct affirmative or negative. She liked to recall a time when she and her mother and her youngest sister Anna were canning green beans. My mother was holding the funnel over the Ball jars, Gram was pouring in the boiling water to sterilize them, and it was Anna's job to say when to stop pouring because the jar was full. "Is it up to the top yet?" Gram asked, and Anna answered, "If it's not quite, it is almost." One day when I came in from the berry patch behind our house and my wife asked if there was any evidence yet of the cooler weather which had been forecast, I said, "Not as far as I can tell." Whatever was wrong with "no," on both those occasions, was also wrong with "yes" at a cookout a few years ago when my cousin Abe was asked whether he thought the chicken ought to be turned over once more on the grill. " It probably wouldn't hurt it any" was his way of saying that he thought it should.

It's not just in my family that this indefinite, indirect answer is preferred to the certain yes or no. Expressions of this sort are and have always been so much a matter of common parlance in northern New England that they're simply taken for granted until we become aware of their singularity and begin to listen for them. Along with particular, distinctive inflections including the sound of the sentence that rises to crescendo in the middle and, having made its assertion, falls off at the end to a quiet emphasis ("Well, I'll tell you, mister man, that horse had his own idea about the situation."), such a manner of speaking is part of what makes me feel, when I have been away from Vermont for a time and have just returned, that I'm home again. It's as native as are the high pastures and stone walls and the taste of pure maple syrup and the blaze of color from the hillsides in October.

This habit of speech, which, it seems to me, somewhat qualifies the northern New Englander's reputation as a man of few words, is much easier to hear than it is to explain. Perhaps it has something to do with life as it is lived in unpredictable extremes of weather and climate which can make solstice and equinox little more than dates on the calendar. That the subject of the weather inspires those speculative, conjectural habits of thought and response in which we Yankees seem to reside most comfortably can be verified early any morning among the men who begin their day at the back of the Teago General Store in South Pomfret. Sitting there in March or April next to the coffee machine with its sign saying "We're probably going to raise our coffee to 50 cents someday" (the store owner at that time, a New Jersey native, had succumbed to the local idiom), even the most definite opinions about whether we have finally come to the end of winter are always cheerfully undercut and concluded with the consensus, "But you never can tell."

On Teago's front steps one cold, overcast November morning, I thought I smelled snow in the air and asked Wayne, the woodsman, if snow was coming. He answered in a string of qualifiers that, to an outsider, would sound more like the beginning than the end of a conversation, "It almost seems as if it might be," and headed for his pickup.

But if to dwell in northern New England is to be subject to whims of climate and weather, it is also to bear witness to the ways in which the natural world adapts to all sorts of extremes and to learn that to bend is not to break. The key seems to be a kind of suppleness in nature that we somehow would be failing to acknowledge were we to take our stand in a definite "yes" or "no" in which there is no room to hedge our bets. Indeed, the happiest and safest position to occupy in the face of contingencies of weather and fortune is that of a thoughtful uncertainty, a position honored by Robert Frost, Vermont's first poet laureate, at the end of "On Looking Up By Chance at the Constellations." Speculating on what even the most dedicated stargazer might gain from his hours of vigilance, Frost's speaker declares that ". . . it wouldn't reward the watcher to stay awake/In hopes of seeing the calm of heaven break/On his particular time and personal sight." Then, as though hearing a little too much unjustified authority and assurance there, he backs up and concludes the thought and the poem in the true Yankee spirit, in which, even in the cosmic scheme of things, possibility is the only certainty: "That calm seems certainly safe to last tonight." And the speaker in Frost's poem "Birches" can be heard doing somewhat the same thing when, after asserting that, "Earth's the right place for love," he seems to hear just a little too much certainty in those words and goes on both to defend that statement and also to leave the door open for a better location should any appear, by adding, "I don't know where it's likely to go better."

If the Yankees' preference for the conjectural over the definite means that they are less likely to be caught unprepared, it also enables them to respond with a sort of graciousness and at the same time to maintain a measure of their proverbial independence. As the answer to an offer or an invitation, their negative is the gentlest of "no's" which both lets you hope that it may turn to an affirmative and leaves them with room to change their mind. When it came time for dessert in our home and my mother would ask my father if he would like a piece of apple pie, his answer of 'not right now, maybe later" was a way of both announcing that he was full and avoiding any sort of implied distrust of her baking skills that "no" might have suggested. Harder to interpret but in the same spirit of courtesy is my uncle's and my brother-in-law's response of "I don't care" to the same sort of offer. Far from expressing apathy or indifference, as it might seem to be doing to the untrained ear, it is perhaps best understood as something like, "well, if there is enough to go around—that is, if there is some left over after everyone has been served—I'd be happy to oblige you." The apparent intention is not to let one's own wish infringe upon the wishes of others. Thus is the indirect affirmative as deferential as the indirect negative.

When conversation turns to discussion, if the northern Yankee doesn't agree with you about something, he sounds as though he doesn't exactly disagree with you either; instead, he politely lets you know that you might be right and, by so doing, keeps the matter open. Not that continued discussion will ever reveal precisely what he truly thinks, for that is *his* affair just as what you are thinking is *your* affair, two separate domains which may overlap, but only consensually. The implied affirmative or negative, then, can take care of what is often the need to let people know that what they have just asked is none of their business without anyone's having to be rude by saying so in so many words. Thus potentially polemical situations are diffused, and the boundaries so necessary to social harmony are maintained by a kind of discourse of implication and appeasement. One long winter in my parents' later years, my father developed the habit of pacing inside their small house. I suppose his repeated circuit of kitchen, front hall, living room, dining room, kitchen, etc. was a combination of restlessness and a way of getting the sort of exercise he needed to keep his circulation going until the weather was warm enough and the ice sufficiently melted to enable him to resume his constitutionals outdoors. My mother, trying to rest on the couch and feeling her nerves increasingly frayed and the house reduced in size with each of his measured, successive orbitings, finally registered her exasperation by asking him, "Have you met anyone on these walks of yours, Wally?" To which he answered, in passing, "Not yet." In those two words, the right of the inquiry was honored, the sarcasm both acknowledged and deflected, and the necessary margin restored to the lives of each. Moreover, the tension was suddenly exploded in shared laughter which included their appreciation of the idiom that had so spontaneously and effectively served the moment.

Ironically, the indirect answer is an example of that restraint by which some of the most cherished Yankee values are acknowledged and protected, as the lexicographer Noah Webster recognized in 1789. Struck by the very different manners of speech in the north and south, he found much to admire in the former:

> In New England, where there are few slaves and servants . . . the people are accustomed to address each other with that diffidence or attention to the opinion of others, which marks a state of equality. Instead of commanding, they advise; instead of saying, with an air of decision, *you must;* they ask with an air of doubtfulness, *is it not best?* or give their opinions with an indecisive tone; *you had better, I believe.*

Thus it is no wonder that a famous twentieth century visitor to New England from the deep south, William Faulkner, was at first baffled by the Yankee reluctance to give a full and direct response. With an ear adapted to the southerners' conversational norm of both candor and disclosure and to what Webster calls "a habit of expressing themselves with a tone of authority and decision," Faulkner was struck by what he considered to be the indifference, if not the downright hostility of Yankee speech. But he eventually came to hear and to admire the same egalitarian spirit that Webster noted, and, realizing that this seeming evasiveness was the very essence of these northern people, he spoke with the deepest respect of "...the men and women themselves so individual, who hold individual integration and privacy as dear as they do liberty and freedom; holding these so high that they take it for granted that all other men and women are individuals, too, and treat them as such, ... with absolute dignity and courtesy."

What is the comparative worth of precision and directness next to such values as these? And the initiated can hear them expressed in even the most casual of exchanges, such as one I overheard some years ago in the Cumberland Farms store in Woodstock, Vermont, the place where I grew up. The son of the woman who was working there as cashier had stopped in at the end of the day to pick up a six-pack and some groceries and to exchange a few words with his mother. As she rang up his purchases, she asked him, "You headed home now, are you?" And I heard him reply in a classic Yankee sentence which allowed for all sorts of unforeseen possibilities and circumstances and changes of heart and at the same time courteously honored the privacy and preserved the freedom of both of them to think what they would: "Oh, I don't know, probably more or less I guess."

Patrimony

The history of one's parents has to be pieced together from fragments, their motives and character guessed at, and the truth about them remains deeply buried, like a boulder that projects one small surface over the level of smooth lawn, and when you come to dig around it, proves too large ever to move, though each year's frost forces it up a little higher. — WILLIAM MAXWELL

1. The Lost Family

On Thanksgiving Day at my Grandmother Coffin's house, my grandfather and his four sons took up most of the space in the small living room that was not occupied by a small center table, three over-stuffed chairs, a couch, a magazine rack, and a large floor model radio. The five of them sat there—clean-shaven, their hair slicked down with hair tonic—and read the newspaper and the magazines or listened to radio newscasts and occasionally spoke to each other and cleared their throats and adjusted their glasses. Though they were situated in the four corners of the room, such were the dimensions that if they had all stood up together, it would have looked something like the beginning of a huddle. And yet they seemed distant from one another. The only space left for my twin brother and me was one end of the couch or a few feet of floor by the door into the front hall, which we occupied for a while, though it was not inviting. Nor was the entire rest of that tall, dark, two-story house at 43 Lincoln Street in Woodstock, Vermont as it was then back in the 1940s and 50s. The woodwork in its small rooms with their high ceilings and in the narrow hallways was stained dark brown and was matched by the wallpaper, which was a dark shade of tan, and complemented by drapes of a dark floral pattern. The paintings and prints hanging on the walls in their heavy, ornate frames seemed to have been chosen to deepen rather than to mitigate the prevailing gloom and the sense of enclosure created by the décor. On the wall above the wide entry way from the dining room to the living room hung a lacquered brown oval piece of wood on which had been painted a string of brown fish hanging on a fishing line. Completely two-dimensional, suspended in no space, they looked trapped, suffocated, as well as dead. My twin brother, Howard, and I (there were just the two of us until our sister Jane was born on our seventh birthday) had little choice but to stay inside with the adults for the entire, long day, though sometimes the cold and barren world outside looked tempting, to me at least. So we quietly looked at scrapbooks or held the View Master up to our eyes like binoculars and worked its trigger to revolve the discs of colored photographs showing historic monuments or national parks. Although Grampa

Coffin sometimes smiled and spoke to us, perhaps to ask us if we liked what we were seeing, his questions and remarks left us very little to say in response. It would never have occurred to us to approach Uncle Jim or Uncle Chick or Uncle Ralph, and evidently they never considered engaging us in any personal way. Something about their not being married and not being fathers made them seem indifferent to us and less avuncular than our uncles on my mother's side of the family.

To escape the sense of claustrophobia given off by the living room, I sometimes climbed the long, banistered staircase in the front hall to explore the rooms upstairs, all of which were so clean, tidy, and austerely furnished as to look as though they were never occupied. In fact, only two of the four bedrooms were regularly used: one by my grandparents, and one by Uncle Jim, my father's older brother. The smallest one, at the top of the stairs, made even smaller by the presence of a large armoire, was reserved for Aunt Lura. She was my grandmother's younger sister who visited once in a while from Hanover, New Hampshire, where she had settled after nurses' training at Mary Hitchcock Hospital and where she worked as a live-in companion to an elderly woman of some means. In the front room my grandparents' double bed with its high, dark wooden headboard took up much of the space not occupied by a large bureau and, in one corner, a small rocking chair without arms. On the walls were a Wallace Nutting photograph of a country scene and a long, low photograph of Shriners, my grandfather included, dressed in their suits and looking very serious for the camera at a state convention. At the end of the hallway was a long, narrow bathroom which smelled of shaving cream,

Lifebuoy soap and disinfectant. In the darkest and most crowded bedroom of all, which my grandmother called "the boys' room," three narrow, beds all tightly made, were situated side by side, barracks style, with little room between them. This was where my father and two of his brothers had slept when they were younger and living at home, and this continued to be Uncle Jim's room. Beyond that, and strangely inviting because you stepped down to enter it and it offered a view of the back lawn, was "Chick's room," at it was still called, though he had not slept there in years. It seemed necessary to be quiet in all those rooms up there, as though I were trespassing, and not to touch things, or if I did, not to leave any traces of my having done so. Perhaps some of the seriousness of the house came from its association with World War II, which had ended three years after Howard and I were born, and in which, in one way or another, all four Coffin boys had served: James Hazen—Haze to his friends and Uncle Jim to us—at a clerical supply detail in the Midwest; Wallace—Wally, as he was called, and my father—in the Vermont State Guard; Chick with the Marines in the Pacific theatre; and Ralph in the Navy aboard aircraft carriers. Their uniforms hung from rafters in the attic and gave off the solemnity of the great Memorial Day parades of that post-war time, though none of them ever marched. The scrapbooks we looked at with my grandmother were filled with pictures of soldiers and tanks and battleships and fighter planes and flagpoles proudly flying the stars and stripes. The heavy end of a mortar shell acted as a doorstop in the dining room, and on top of an armoire in the boys' room was Chick's bayonet, strapped into a leather sheath and still razor sharp, something we were never to touch and high up enough to be well out of our reach.

For some years, when I was very young, the "boys' room" was the room that I was so afraid of that I was uneasy being upstairs there at all, even in my mother's company. What frightened me was a portrait photo in black and white that hung on the wall across from the three beds. It showed a young woman, from the neck up, with her hair arranged somewhat in cameo fashion; she was posing with her head turned slightly to her left so that her whole face was in view but at an angle. Since she was of pale complexion similar to the blank space she occupied in the frame, somehow I thought she was looking at me and trying to draw me into that flat white space that surrounded her and was infecting her with its pallor. My fear was compounded by the uneasiness it seemed to arouse in those who learned of it. The woman in the picture was evidently not to be discussed, as though there was something forbidden about her. My father had no patience at all with any fearful mention of "that lady" as I called her. My grandmother, in some embarrassment, went so far as to cover the portrait with a cloth in preparation for our visits, but that simply convinced me she was hiding back there, lurking just out of sight. My mother told me in private that the woman was the mother of my father and his brothers, and the picture was there so that they could see and remember her. She had died years before Howard and I were born. She was, as I came to understand later, greatly loved by her sons, though they never spoke of her. What I learned about her came from what my father had told my mother. Her name was Mildred Anthony, the surname being that of her adoptive parents. She loved music and played the organ at the Christian Church, near their home on Pleasant Street, and she evidently was warm and had a wonderful sense of humor and loved good fun. How she met my grandfather I do not know, but their marriage certificate tells me that on November 2, 1902 she and Clarence Coffin were married in the old Methodist Church in Woodstock. She bore five sons: James Hazen in 1904, Wallace Burbank in 1907, Charles Franklin in 1911, Howard Anthony in 1916, and Ralph Edson in 1923. Howard's birth had been difficult for her, and she had been diagnosed with Bright's disease by that time. My wife recalls being told by my mother that the doctors made it clear to her and to my grandfather that as a result of her illness there should be no more children. However, six years later at the age of 44 she became pregnant and gave premature birth to Ralph in June of 1923. She died four months later in October of that year—a month after her six-year old-son Howard was struck by an automobile and killed—leaving her husband and her remaining four sons bereft and unmoored. My uncles never spoke of this time in their lives, and my father, sometimes when Howard and I were alone with him as children, would begin to do so but couldn't get much beyond letting us know that he had once had a little brother about our age and he was named Howard too, and then his voice would become thick, and he would find no words and would take out his handkerchief, ostensibly to blow his nose but also, we noticed, to wipe his eyes. Then, after a silence, the best he could do was to tell us that we must always look both ways before crossing the street. My father told my mother early in their relationship that when he was only sixteen years old, he had shed so many tears that for the rest of his life, there would be no more.

Shut away in her picture upstairs, Mildred was never mentioned; no references were ever made at Thanksgiving to her place in the family. These occasions belonged entirely to her successor, Bertha Metcalf, my grandfather's second wife, and she provided a feast. By early afternoon at the latest, the nine of us would be called to our customary places at the table covered with her best linen table cloth and her best set of china. As bachelors, my uncles seldom saw a table so sumptuously laden, and they all had large appetites and heaped their plates with turkey, stuffing, boiled potatoes smothered in gravy, green beans, squash, carrots, boiled onions, and cranberry sauce. And after that, they somehow found room for apple pie and pumpkin pie, which they ate with large pieces of sharp cheddar cheese. The main business of the day was, clearly, eating, though I recall some conversation, usually started by Uncle Jim. Perhaps because he lived there, he always seemed more relaxed and at home than the rest of them. My father, there with his brothers and talking to them, seemed unusually distant to us in his place across the table. My mother too seemed somewhat out of reach where she sat; she would participate, though she was not, I noticed, the lively and spontaneous person we saw in our little apartment on Pleasant Street and in her parents' warm and noisy farmhouse in South Pomfret with her brothers and sisters and nephews and nieces. Nevertheless, she was careful to tip me a wink from time to time to let me know I hadn't been forgotten and that she too was making the best of the situation there until we'd be back home. Once in a while, Howard or I might say something, but, outnumbered as we were, it was not easy to feel all that attention focused on us by people we didn't know very well. It was best just to eat and to study my uncles, who seemed in some ways much alike and at the same time very different from each other. My father and Uncle Jim took up less space than their younger brothers, not only because they were slighter in build but also because they spoke more softly and more slowly. They wore the same wire-rimmed glasses and showed the same kind of quiet self-possession. They were in the center of what conversation took place during the meal. Chick and Ralph seemed more ill at ease, and less patient with any questions my grandmother might ask them about their lives. Chick was broad-shouldered and heavy and guarded. Though he was not much connected to what was being discussed or remarked upon, his voice was more stentorian so that his remarks would sound like retorts or challenges. And his eyes always fascinated me. They were blue like all his brothers' and most like my father's, with the downward slope toward the cheekbones but exaggeratedly so, giving him somehow an expression that was at once both sad and defiant. One almost expected to see, and sometimes inexplicably did see, tears there. And he had a way of regarding Howard and me that was both suspicious and amused as though he had our number and assumed we were plotting something or had been up to some mischief that he quite approved of. Ralph, the youngest, always seemed happy to be with his brothers. His voice was the loudest and the strangest of those heard around the table. It was peculiarly adenoidal and always sounded as if his nose, which was larger than the prominent Coffin nose of his brothers, and hooked, was stuffed up. His head, which rose to a sort of point, had a shape that was unique in the family. He had the sloped blue Coffin eyes, but they were livelier than Chick's, and his manner was more animated. Once in a while when he would catch me studying him, he would give me a quick raise of the head and an amused half smile, and he seemed, in a callous sort of way, to be intrigued with us, his nephews, the two small boys at the table with the grownups, where he, who was only in his late twenties, would otherwise have been the youngest one. My grandfather was always the only one of the men to be dressed up. He wore a three-piece suit and watch chain, necktie, and starched shirts, his well-trimmed gray hair neatly combed and parted. He was the quietest of all; he listened, sometimes made a comment, always asked for someone to pass "the French apples" when he wished for the potatoes, but otherwise seemed to be a guest, much like his sons, rather than a resident in the house.

Though everyone was beholden to my grandmother for her generosity and all her efforts, it would be wrong to call those Thanksgiving dinners festive, for the conversation was laconic, and there was little laughter. After the meal was over, the men would repair to their chairs in the living room to snooze or listen to the radio, and my mother and grandmother would do the washing up and then spend some time with us at the card table putting puzzles together or playing Chinese checkers, neither of which interested me. Then, as the afternoon drew on, Ralph and Chick would each announce that he had better be going along, and Uncle Jim would usually leave for Gray

Camp in Barnard, as it was hunting season. So the brothers would disband and would not be all together again until the next Thanksgiving. Since my sister Jane was too young to remember these holidays, there is no record of them now except in the memories of Howard and me. No one ever brought a camera to record them. There are no Coffin family photographs as such, and it is even hard to imagine my father and his brothers getting together by themselves or with my grandparents to have their pictures taken. Not that they would have objected if anyone had requested a snapshot, but I doubt that they would have felt comfortable posing, and I don't think any of them would have considered it a true family photo. For to them, it would have recorded a giant absence, that of Mildred, "that lady," on the wall upstairs, my grandfather's first wife, mother to the five boys and our true grandmother. And in her place, occupying the vacuum, would have been Bertha Metcalf, stepmother to the boys and the only paternal grandmother we ever knew. As I realized many years later, they were a family without a center, citizens of a foreign country to which they could never fully adapt; the lives they made for themselves were in some ways those of refugees from a homeland that had disappeared, and dispersal seemed more natural to them than convocation. Perhaps that is why it is easier for me to see my uncles with their coats on standing at the back door, saying goodbye, than it is to see them arriving or even seated in the living room or at their positions around the dinner table. In leaving, they seemed to me simply to be obeying the impulse that I felt so strongly, for once the winter sun began to decline and the living room and dining room curtains were drawn and the lamps were switched on, accentuating the shadows along the high ceilings and in the corners and making the front hall too dark to enter and the narrow pantry seem haunted, all I could think about was going home. Even my grandfather seemed to share in that pervasive sentiment; as one after the other of his sons thanked my grandmother and bade farewell, he would begin to lose some of his customary reserved demeanor and, with tears in his eyes, he would tell them he was sorry they had to leave and hoped they would come again soon. He was particularly saddened by our departure, and it was clear that my grandmother and my mother and father found these displays of emotion embarrassing and unseemly, unsuitable, particularly for Howard and me, who looked to my mother in some confusion. Considering it now from an age close to what his was at that time, I think his sadness was a kind of homesickness that was always present in all of them, but held well in check by his sons, and that its expression was a violation of a tacit code of stoicism that they all had accepted. How much my grandmother understood of all this, I do not know. She was in many ways a straight-laced Victorian lady with a very well-formed sense of propriety and a great deal of authority, and it was, I suppose, largely her sense of duty that inspired her to bring together my grandfather and his sons for that one day every year. And whatever her understanding of its success or failure as such, her greatest reward was to spend time with us, her grandsons, and to know that she had done what the head of any family ought to do on Thanksgiving in her own house, just as she had done all that she had it in her to do to make her house a home for her husband and his sons, whether they accepted it as such or not.

For me, those long days in that house with the displaced and distant people of my father's family were redeemed only by my mother's sympathetic presence and the certainty that she shared my sense of isolation. I grew up assuming that fathers were not to be as well known as mothers, and in my childhood and youth, I saw little to suggest the contrary. It was not simply that from infancy on my personality—indeed, my very consciousness itself—was shaped in the quiet presence of my mother while my father was off at work. Mothers listened and understood, and fathers came home at the end of the day and, however doting and responsible, divided the attention and somehow broke the spell. Growing up, I was always more my mother's than my father's child. She so lit up my world and is still at times so present to me that I could no more describe her accurately than I could gaze directly at the sun. Not so my father, who, by contrast, seemed somehow to withhold himself from me and was my "other" parent, just as in the short time they knew him, he was for my children the "other" grandparent, as his father had been for Howard and Jane and me. It was not just that my mother's longer life—she was eight years younger than my father, and she survived him by seventeen years—enabled my daughter Lizzie and my son Jonathan to come to know her and answer her love with a love of their own. She lived almost entirely to serve others. This is not to suggest that my father was in any way too self-concerned or absent or harsh or irresponsible in his paternal role. In fact, once he became a father, he all but gave up any sort of social life he had enjoyed to devote himself entirely to his family. Physically, he was by today's standards, a small man, around five feet seven inches in height and of slight build, but he had immense presence, something that made him seem all the more set apart and reserved and private. He also had a great heart, but except for moments which rendered him almost completely defenseless, that heart was much of the time in hiding. It was not until I married and began having children myself that I discovered my father in myself and came to wonder whether the unknowable part of him and his brothers somehow lay buried in that dark period of 1923 and its aftermath, and whether some excavation of that time might bring me closer to them and enable me to give to my children, whose lives barely overlapped with theirs, some sense of who those Coffin men really were. And since none of my father's three brothers produced children (a legacy perhaps of their early losses?), it seemed as though it was up to me to find out what I could and to tell their story.

Who my grandfather Coffin was as a young married man and as a father and what his life with his young family was like are matters that are now far beyond any living memory, though Howard and I made one attempt several years ago at what we saw as our last chance to talk to someone who had known the Coffin family in those early times. Clara Richardson was related through marriage to the Gillingham family and worked as a bookkeeper for most of her long life at F. H. Gillingham and Sons, the dry goods store where my grandfather worked for fifty-two years. She had known him and Mildred back then, and she had known Bertha Metcalf as well. Some years after

Clara retired from the store, she agreed to talk to Howard and me about the old days, and we went to see her at her house on lower Lincoln Street one winter afternoon. She was a small, thin, gray-haired woman in her 80s at that time, with bright eyes and a quick mind, reminiscent of the actress Katie Johnson in her role as Mrs. Wilberforce in the 1950s British film *The Lady Killers*. For anyone in search of the past, her house seemed a good place to find it. Much of the space in the kitchen was taken up by the same sort of Glenwood stove that I remember from my childhood times at my grandparents' house, and the living room we were shown into had the same sort of stuffed chairs and magazine racks. Old family photographs stared at us from ancient frames, the light from the table lamps glinted off glass figurines and painted dishes in the large china cabinet, and the house was overheated. After some pleasant conversation, Howard, who was a journalist at the time and had done a great deal of interviewing, reminded Clara that we were interested in learning something more about our real grandmother, whom we had never known, and he began by asking Clara to describe Mildred Anthony as she remembered her. Both of us were equipped with pens and notebooks, and, unbeknownst to Clara, we had also smuggled in a small tape recorder, which Howard had managed to sequester, half-concealed under his coat on the floor next to his chair. As Clara began speaking, he waited until she was looking away and then slowly leaned to the side and pressed the start button. Somehow hearing the small click from all the way across the room where she was sitting, she stopped speaking, mid-sentence, and asked in mild alarm, "Oh, what was that?"

Howard, disconcerted, explained that it was a tape recorder and that her recollections were so important to us that we wanted to make sure we didn't miss a thing. Clara replied, "We won't be needing that." Chastised, Howard said, "Oh, OK," and switched it off. Just then, her telephone rang in the kitchen, and when she went to answer it, Howard watched her until she was out of sight, and then, looking straight at me with a belligerent expression in which I read, "Don't try to bully me, old lady," leaned over and jammed his finger down on the starter button as though assaulting it, and the rest of the interview was recorded. As it turned out, he need not have bothered, for we learned very little from Clara: "Mildred was a lovely lady, and she and Clarence were a happy couple, and as the boys came along, they all made a happy family. No, they didn't have a lot of money, I suppose, but life was simpler back then, and they made do with what they had," and so on, without any of the small individualizing details that can suddenly bring forth a vanished world and illuminate a human personality.

Though we thanked Clara effusively for her time and memories—Howard jocularly remarking that indeed we had not needed the tape recorder—our sense was that the interview had been a failure. So much so that we never bothered playing it back, and eventually the tape was discarded or lost. Oddly enough, it seemed to me that our time there with her had brought back the wrong grandmother—Bertha, and not Mildred. Like Bertha, Clara, in spite of her diminutive stature, was formidable. What made Howard and me too timid to ask her permission to record our session and prompted our furtive acts of deception was the same puritanical capacity for stern disapproval which could make her presence, all evident graciousness and hospitality aside, seem somehow unwelcoming. Even in Howard's defiant expression as he punched the recorder back on in Clara's absence, I was reminded of some of Chick and Ralph's blunt, monosyllabic retorts to Bertha's questions at Thanksgiving. But as we were leaving Clara's house that day, stepping out into the gray winter afternoon on her front porch, she said something, off the record, as it were, that was to prove strangely indelible: "I remember so well the day of Mildred's funeral at the Christian Church, seeing those boys with Clarence and thinking 'now they have no mother.'"

Though it caught my attention at the time, this image of my grandfather, the widower, with his motherless sons, was not enough to keep me searching for the Coffin family. Howard and I had tapped what we considered to be our only source of living memories and had discovered nothing of any real value. We had come up empty, and I regretted that we had not begun our investigation years earlier. Too much time had passed; too many people had disappeared and taken with them the times we were looking for; the moment and the opportunity had been lost. What I didn't understand then is that the times and the conditions for what we need to know are determined less by our wishes and intentions than by our lives as such. Could we by some reversal or jaunt in a time machine go back to the years and the people we seek, we would find ourselves and them to be just as we had been, in the familiar relationships which both reveal and constrict what we can know about each other. Had I begun my inquiry when my father and his brothers were still living, I doubt I could have brought myself to ask them direct questions about their past, for it would have seemed some kind of trespass, a violation of the ways in which we were present to each other. It wasn't more of the past I needed, but more of the future, other voices, other rooms. I needed to be carried much further forward in order to find my way back—forward into, among other things, the experience of fatherhood and the promptings from my children which began to give me a strange sense of identity with my father and to recast the experience of family so as to make it necessary to go looking for him.

In marrying and having children, I was making the choice that my father alone of his generation of Coffins had made. And, like him, I started a family in my 30s. My second child, Jonathan—the last of the five grandchildren and the only name bearer—was born when my father was 71, so Wallace Coffin and Jonathan Coffin met only in passing, so to speak, and had less than four years together. Nevertheless, although Jonathan is not able to distinguish what may be a memory of my father from what he has been told about him, somehow they seem to have bonded. The first evidence of this came from the last time they were together. Unlike his older sister, Elizabeth (Lizzie), Jonathan did not begin talking at an early age, and he had difficulty in making himself understood and used to become angry and frustrated in his attempts to do so. He had no name for my father until suddenly, in my father's hospital room, not many days before his death, he began speaking to him and of him as "Wally." It was almost as though he were saying to his sister and his parents and his grandmother, "He may be

'Grampa' and 'Poppa' to you, but he and I, as pals, are on a first name basis." And not long after that, on the cold and overcast day of my father's funeral in early January of 1983, Jonathan once again had his own response. After the service at the North Pomfret Church, rather than driving directly back to Lincoln Street, we decided to go to Riverside Cemetery where my father was being taken for burial. We arrived just at the moment when the casket was being lowered into the grave. The low layer of cloud was threatening to bring the short day to an early end, and the two inches of snow on the ground and the gravestones seemed to be supplying what little light there was. When we explained to the children that Grampa was going to a long rest there, Jonathan, evidently thinking it would be warm and cozy snuggled up next to him under the snow, told us he wanted to go with him.

Many years later, when Jonathan was in his twenties and working his way through college in Cambridge, Massachusetts, I witnessed a similar meeting of him and his grandfather. I mentioned to him that Poppa, as we called him, after graduating from Woodstock High School in 1925, had spent a year doing a course of study at Wentworth Institute in Boston. I remembered him taking Howard and me—when we were ten years old and in Boston for our first Red Sox game and a look around the city—to his old Back Bay neighborhood to show us where he had lived. And I was fortunate enough to find in the house at Lincoln Street the address of his apartment—65 Astor Street—and to remember his telling me that the name of the street had been changed since he had lived there to Burbank Street (ironically, as my father's middle name, it became the source of a family joke about his fame). One Saturday in October, after some search, Jonathan and I discovered the quiet street and, in a block of three and four-story residential buildings, #65. Its stone front steps leading up to a large portico and front door awakened a vague recollection of my first visit to that site some fifty years before. The address I had discovered specified suite 14 as his, and we wondered what floor that was located on and what features in the neighborhood would have changed in the view from his windows. It was a bright fall day, and we wandered off in the blowing leaves, eventually coming upon a short street with benches at the end. By that time, we had gotten away from the subject of my father and were talking, as I recall, about classical music when, after a pause, Jonathan, whose mind evidently had not wandered, suddenly said, "Just think, Dad, he might have walked right along this sidewalk past this place where we are now." There they were again, two generations that had barely touched, reaching across me to reaffirm their connection and give me a strange and wavering image of their actually being there together for the first time as adults in my absence with myself instead of my father as the invisible onlooker. This moment, perhaps more than any other, told me that if Jonathan's sense of family connection was this strong already, it would no doubt grow stronger when he had married and had children, and therefore I had better help him find out all I could about his forebears before I passed on and left him with unanswered questions.

Most of what we have come to know about the lost family my brother and I had hoped to find by interviewing Clara

Richardson was discovered some years later in a trunk tucked back under the eaves in the cluttered attic of the house at Lincoln Street. It was a box of letters to Uncle Jim from his family in the fall of 1922 when he was away for a post-graduate year at Tilton School in Tilton, New Hampshire. These letters—most of them were written by his mother and father, but there are also a few from his brothers Wallace and Chick— provide the only picture of the Coffin family before the birth of Ralph in June of 1923 and the death of Howard in September followed by the death of the boys' mother only a month later. In fact, the postmarks of the letters sent in early December are very close to the time when Millie, as she was called, must have realized that she was, against the dire warning of the doctors, pregnant once again and facing grave danger in the months ahead if her condition worsened, as it might very well do in the course of carrying the child and giving birth. Though she was already suffering from the disease that would prove fatal, what she writes, with the exception of one brief mention of her illness, suggests that she was still able to lead a full life and to keep up a lively and affectionate correspondence with her oldest son, who was experiencing his first time away from home and was very much missed by his parents and his brothers. "Dear Hazen," she writes in a letter from October, "How I would like to see you. It seems a long time since you went away." And on November 21, "How I would like to slip in and see you. I think we could say a whole lot." In another letter, "How I would like to get hold of you and give you a big hug." Although none of his letters survive, it is obvious that Haze wrote often, reporting regularly on his daily experiences at boarding school and inquiring about the details of life at home and about the general events in Woodstock. Ever mindful of what their son might enjoy or need in his time away from home, his parents sent him issues of the *Vermont Standard* to keep him up on the news, a new pair of socks, the scatter rug from his room, his napkin ring, a dollar or two. Their letters show a reverence for the common things of their life, including their animals. They kept a cow in the small barn at the back of their house on Pleasant Street, and also chickens, including "five Rhode Island Red hens," and there are notations of the number of eggs they were producing. Millie keeps Haze informed on the activities of the much-loved family dog: "Beauty is fine. She is getting to be a great hunter. She brought in a flying gray squirrel the other night and Pa couldn't get it out until morning when he found him sitting on top of the trout picture. He was beautiful, so soft." And then there were the horses. Though his work at Gillingham's required my grandfather to take care of the horses used for the delivery route which he drove every day, such was his love of them that he was not averse to hitching one of them up again on a weekend for the kind of family outing he greatly enjoyed; Millie reports, "Last night Pa hitched Lady up and gave Howard and me a moonlight ride." And my grandfather mentions that he "had Lady clipped yesterday. This afternoon gave Mother a ride and let her step along, seemed as young as she did 15 years ago." In the winter, after "the sleighs [were] all painted and ready for snow," there were family sleigh rides. In spite of his busy work schedule, my grandfather always found time for his wife and children. Even after attending the required "store meetings," which sometimes lasted until late at night, he would be able to add a cheerful greeting in his letter to Haze next morning early before dropping it in the post on his way to work. Then too there are the unfailing touches of good humor in the letters of both parents and in the letters from my sixteen-year-old father, who addresses his brother as "you old stocking" and cautions him not to "eat too many beans bottom side up lest you get hiccups." He keeps him updated on the results of after-school football games played with friends and tells him about their mischief on Halloween. Evidently, it was expected that all Tilton students would do a turn at waiting on table in the school dining room. A letter of Millie's suggests that her son had reported an accident that had occurred on one of the evenings when he was the waiter. In her unfailing equanimity, which he must have experienced as loving and supportive, she says, "Perhaps we'll get a bill for the broken dishes. I'd like to have seen your face when you dropped the tray." His father asks him about "all the pretty girls at Tilton," and Millie tells him, "I've made five apple pies this week. They don't go quite so fast since you left." She also tells him, regarding Woodstock's annual Windsor County Fair, that, according to a family friend, "he didn't have to crawl off the fair grounds this year because they have made a rule that people don't have to get drunk."

Read by someone with no knowledge of the Coffins, these letters might have their interest as a picture of family life in the Woodstock of the early twentieth century. It was a quiet time when evenings might be spent playing cards or entertaining friends—"We invited Warren and Elizabeth [Gillingham], Mr.

and Mrs. Marcott and Clara [Richardson] down and had two tables of Whist"—or having "a gramophone concert," or going out to "the pictures" or to a church supper, "65 cents a plate"; a time when preparation for winter included the purchase of a barrel of apples, the installation of storm windows, and the necessary delivery of a load of coal to the cellar. The letters depict a period of transition to the modern world in their reference to modes of transportation and commerce: the Woodstock Railway, though at that time in its last decade of service, was still a means of conveyance for freight and passengers, as we are reminded by my grandfather's advising his son to pack a lunch for December 15, the day when he would be traveling home from Tilton for Christmas, because "the trains are running late every afternoon and Saturday traffic will be extra heavy." And his mother's mentioning to him that "the train has just whistled in" is a reminder that trains would have been heard regularly arriving and departing by anyone the village at that time, as would the clip-clop of horses in what was nearly the end of their long day in the affairs of men. For the automobile in its early forms had made its incursion, as the letters remind us—"one of the boys in Wallace's class broke his arm cranking his car on Wednesday." At least to Clarence and Mildred Coffin, born as they were in 1879, automobiles were still enough of a novelty to take note of, as they do in referring to the sight and sound of cars going by their house. So large is the shadow cast back across the letters by Howard's untimely passing that even something as incidental as the juxtaposition of horse-drawn conveyance and automobile projects the image of the small boy stepping down out of the security and safety of the one into the fatal path of the other. In fact, the time signatures above the details of the Coffins' daily life as recorded are so pervasive as to bear by themselves the theme of transience which sounds in all the letters, and which, to the knowing reader, carries such a deep sense of pathos. Millie's letter of October 11, noting that "the leaves are falling fast, our yard is covered with the yellow ones," speaks of a seasonal event she may well be witnessing for the last time, and her twentieth wedding anniversary, which, she reminds her son, will be occurring on November 25th, will be her last. Clarence's letter of December 4, reminding Haze that "Howard is six tomorrow" unknowingly records his youngest son's last birthday, as does Millie's news that the birthday presents included " a snow shovel, five hdkfs [handkerchiefs], some money, an auto wind up, and a fire engine," and she mentions that, as it had snowed two inches the day before, "his shovel has had a good trial so far." There is, as well, a kind of poignancy in Clarence and Millie's tendency to close their letters to their first-born with an accounting of the family's whereabouts: from Millie—"Howard is in the land of nod, Wallace has gone to the pictures, and Chick is in the barn with Dad"; and from Clarence—"Mother and Chick just gone to church, Wallace reading, and Howard asleep." It is as though they are at once assuring Haze that all persons are secure and accounted for and expressing a grateful acceptance for the presence of so much that has been given to them.

By the spring of 1923, the picture of life in the Coffin family had darkened. During this time, Millie, pregnant with Ralph and suffering from Bright's disease, which was beginning to weaken her heart, evidently—as a post card to her husband indicates—underwent a period of treatment at the State Sanatorium in Rutland, Massachusetts. When she returns home, consensus is that she was released too soon. Her mother—Granma Anthony as she calls herself—who had by now come to live with them and help out in the house, tells Haze, "She came home before she should have," and Clarence reports that the family doctor, Dr. Eastman, "was surprised and also provoked because she was home so soon." From this time forward, Clarence as correspondent clearly feels it his duty to assure his son by giving the best possible reports of his mother's health: "Mother is gaining slowly, able to walk to the bathroom, sits up about half the day, eats all she ought to and sleeps very good." And a week or so later, evidently in answer to some concern on his son's part, he tells him, "Don't feel anxious about her as she is doing very well and is in good spirits." At the same time, Granma Anthony apparently wants her grandson to know something about the seriousness of his mother's condition: "Friday night she had a bad spell. We sent for Dr. E. and he was very much frightened and said she must go to bed and stay there and have a nurse to look after her. Now she is in bed and fixed very comfortable, so don't you worry. But I thought I should inform you a little, so if anything happens it won't come on you too sudden." It may very well have been Haze's distress over this report that led him to consider dropping out of Tilton not long before he was scheduled to graduate in order to come home to be with his family and do what he could for them all. His distress prompted his father to reassure him and encourage him to finish his schooling: "Just rest easy about affairs up here. You don't want to be a quitter so near the end of the school year." And as Haze's mind may have been very much on the well-being of his little brother in this time of their mother's suffering, his father tells him, "Mother sleeps in our bed, I sleep with Howard."

If the devastating events that shattered the lives of all of them were never mentioned in any letters that have come to light, they must, it seemed to me, have been recorded at the time they occurred in Woodstock's town newspaper. By the time Jonathan and I decided to consult the old issues of the *Vermont Standard,* my recollection of what I had heard from my father and mother was not much better than that of my brother, who at one time was under the impression that his namesake had died in a sledding accident at the bottom of Ford Street or Stanton Street. On the afternoon in the Woodstock History Center when we were handed the great bound copy of the 1923 *Standards,* we had the entire reading room to ourselves, and we progressed slowly, as I like to do when going back into history in this way, making my way forward by looking at the headlines, spotting the names of old familiar families in wedding and birth announcements and obituaries, noticing houses referred to by occupants rather than by street number, perusing old ads from Gillingham's and other stores and sharing some of Jonathan's astonishment at the prices of things back then. By the time we had reached June and discovered the announcement of Ralph's birth, I had begun to feel something of the old village of Woodstock as referred to in my grandparents' letters to their son taking shape around us. Turning the pages from week to week, we came to the autumn of 1923, and in the issues of September 13 and September 20 we found what we were looking for:

> Howard Anthony Coffin, the six-year-old son of Mr. and Mrs. Clarence F. Coffin of Pleasant Street, died Wednesday afternoon of last week in Hanover Hospital as the result of having been hit by an automobile on Pleasant Street in the morning of the same day. The lad was with his father on one of the Gillingham order teams, which stopped in front of W. H. Reed's house, and Mr. Coffin was across the street at J. S. Brownell's residence. Suddenly the lad jumped from the team and started across the street toward his father and was hit by a passing machine, and taken to the hospital, never regaining consciousness.

And then follows a more exact account of the accident, given in the kind of investigative detail and curiously graphic language of newspaper reporting of that time:

> The circumstances of the lamentable accident were as follows: Mr. Coffin had stopped on the right side of the street as noted and went across to Mr. Brownell's, leaving his young son in the wagon. A procession of three motor cars came from down the street, keeping to the middle to pass the team. Meanwhile Frank K. Knapp with his car had started upstreet from the railway station. As the last of the

three downward cars passed the wagon young Howard Coffin left the team and darted across the street
to join his father; and as the Knapp car came along
just then within three or four feet of the rear car
down-ward, the lad before he could stop himself ran
into it, striking the fender above the forward wheel.
He put his hands up to save himself but was too late,
and the fender cut a gash in his forehead. He was
thrown backward onto the hard-surfaced street and
rendered unconscious, suffering a fracture of the
skull. Dr. Eastman was summoned, the boy having
been carried into the Brownell house, and false respi-
ration restored his breathing. He was taken at once
to Hanover Hospital in W. B. Gilchrist's car, accom-
panied by Dr. Eastman, and was still unconscious
when they departed.

Granma Anthony's letter to Haze had informed him that,
"Howard rides with his father quite a little," no doubt because
his mother was too ill to take care of him, and thus he must
often have been with his father on his morning delivery
rounds. What prompted young Howard to leave the wagon
will, of course, never be known. I suppose it was my grandfather who knelt down in the street and picked him up and
carried him into the Brownell house. Or maybe he was so
much in shock that someone else, Mr. Brownell or Frank
Knapp himself or a witness to the accident, did it. When I try
to imagine being my grandfather in those moments, I can't do
it. Even without my familiarity with the place, which tells me

within inches of the exact spot where Howard was struck
down and gives to the accident a terrible immediacy, the
newspaper account has a way of undoing its reader, as was the
case with Jonathan. There at our table in the Woodstock
History Center where he was reading to me and I was taking
dictation, I realized from his stopping more often than he had
been when he was adjusting to the speed of my writing that the
lump in his throat was making it difficult for him to keep
going. The accident occurred no more than two hundred yards
east of the Coffin family home at that time on Pleasant Street
where Mildred was confined to her bed, but it was my grandfather who had to deliver to her the terrible news. According to
my mother, he did not at once tell her what had happened.
Removed from her infant son Ralph, who had been sent to live
with and be reared by a farm family in Quechee, Vermont
because she was too ill to care for him, she must have been in
danger of weakening herself with great worries about the
present and future of her husband and sons. As her physical
condition deteriorated (the letters report the family's and the
doctor's concern about keeping her quiet because "she is very
nervous and doesn't lie down much"), my grandfather may well
have feared that the news of Howard's death would prove fatal
to her. However, when he had summoned the courage to enter
the house and make his way to their bedroom, his best efforts
to keep her from learning that something dreadful had occurred proved futile. As my mother evidently heard it from my
father, Millie took one look at him and said, "It's Howard, isn't
it? Something has happened to Howard."

Howard's funeral took place four days after his death. In the words of the *Vermont Standard,* it was "largely attended on Saturday afternoon in the Christian Church. It was held there on account of the serious illness of the lad's mother at home." The suggestion here is that Millie was not able to attend the service. As Jonathan and I were reading and recording these events, we could not escape the impression that the Coffin family had been strangely shadowed by tragic circumstances; nor, evidently, could the people of Woodstock at that time, as reported: "The community is deeply stirred by sympathy for these good people on account of this bereavement and also because misfortunes of ill health and accident have seemed to dwell with them persistently in the past few years." That sympathy must have deepened when, less than a month later on Sunday, October 7, Millie died. Her obituary speaks of her as "ever a lover of home and family," and ends with the information that she "leaves beside her husband and mother four of her five sons as well as a large circle of friends to sincerely mourn her loss." Something of the nature and extent of the townspeople's support is indicated in the news that "the junior class and the officers of the other classes attended the funeral of Mrs. Clarence Coffin . . . as a mark of respect toward their classmate and school-fellow Wallace Coffin." No doubt many of the classmates of Uncle Jim, who had graduated in 1922, would have been there as well.

I imagine that after the death of his son and his wife, survival for my grandfather and his family meant somehow putting what had been his life behind him and moving on. If in some ways he never fully recovered, as I believe he didn't, his failure to do so may have been as much the result of guilt as it was of sorrow. Uncle Jim told my mother once that he was never able to forgive his father for getting his mother pregnant that last time after being told not to do so. Whether my father and Chick felt the same way, I do not know; nor do I know whether my grandfather could forgive himself. And he may very well have blamed himself in some way for the death of Howard, who was his responsibility on the day he was killed. At any rate, he must have realized not long after his wife's death that, with his job at Gillingham's, he would have great difficulty in raising his sons without some help. As much as I would like to think of his second marriage, four years later in 1927, as a sign of recovery, I see it primarily as a kind of capitulation, a surrender to the urgent requirements of the present. I suppose the woman who became his second wife, Bertha Metcalf, was among "the large circle of friends" referred to in the newspaper, and that she knew the Coffin family very well. Millie's obituary mentions her involvement in "the woman's Relief Corps and in the King's Daughters," organizations to which Bertha belonged, and both of them were members of the Christian Church. The *Standard's* announcement of Howard's death states that "a movement which started quite spontaneously from various sources promises a testimonial of sympathy which will be quite tangible and substantial," and I can well imagine that Bertha's relationship with my grandfather began with her part in that testimonial. Their marriage, which one might assume signified the inclusion of his new wife in the life of the Coffin family, has always seemed to me to be the reverse: the life of the Coffins as it had been was over, and my grandfather and his sons were given a place in Bertha's house and in her life. The family home, such as it was, on Pleasant Street was given up, and Clarence, Haze, Wally, Chick, and eventually Ralph moved into her house, the Metcalf house, at 43 Lincoln Street. What I see as her attempted rescue operation was no doubt prompted by compassion for the boys, and she may very well have loved my grandfather. There is a passage in a novel by Ivan Doig in which a widower, Oliver Milliron, with a number of motherless children explains his immunity to women since the death of his wife, and his intention not to marry again: "I will not go through life resenting a woman because she isn't Florence . . . and a stepmother for this tribe of heathens is apt to be a curse worse than the affliction." The situation imagined here is, I think, in some ways what the Coffins found in their life with Bertha and what she found with them, and had my grandfather been gifted with Milliron's prescience, the lives of his sons, at least, might have been quite different.

For my grandfather, the marriage must have seemed a solution to the problem of his motherless family. For Bertha it was a way out of a lonely and austere spinsterhood. She had lived there by herself on Lincoln Street, and between her parents' death and her marriage to Clarence, in what must have been the worst of times, she took in boarders and worked as their cook and chambermaid. She slept in the attic, where today her bed with its tall, Victorian headboard of dark oak, the circular stovepipe hole in the chimney, and the porcelain chamber pot are grim testimonials to the straitened circumstances which she managed as best she could. Un-insulated as it was in those days, that attic must have tested the powers of her small coal stove and kerosene heater, which were her only defenses against the cold on winter nights at the top of the house, and in that tinderbox the lack of any fire escape except the perilously steep attic stairs to the second floor was quite likely a constant worry. Though she was, I believe, a brave and indomitable woman, I can only suppose that she was somewhat daunted by the prospect of stepping into Millie's place as wife and mother. At least, I would like to think she was, because such self-doubts are, after all, only human, and they would help to soften my memories of her and inspire me to return in some greater measure the love she felt for Howard and me, her grandsons. As Howard recalls, she once told my mother that she had desperately wanted children of her own. To her, we, rather than her stepsons, were the children she never had, and she went out of her way to do everything she could for us. So much so that my parents thought she went overboard by providing us with too much. Every year on Christmas morning, the living room in our small apartment on Pleasant Street would be more than half-filled with gifts from her, starting at the base of the Christmas tree in the corner and fanning outward in a single and even double layer across the rug. Somehow my father and Uncle Jim would have managed to bring them all down from Lincoln Street and to set them up on Christmas Eve after we had gone to bed. Then she and my grandfather would appear half way through Christmas morning to experience with us our happiness at receiving all that we had wanted and more.

Over and above all, Grammy Coffin, as we called her, did for us, we often heard how much she cared for us. When my mother or father or even Uncle Jim spoke of her after her death, they would sometimes add, "my, how she loved you boys." But on the rare occasions when Chick and Ralph mentioned her to us, the tone was different, clearly meaning that we darned well ought to be glad she loved us that well. For whatever she had envisioned as her role in assuming their mother's place in the Coffin family, the experience of these younger boys was that love was not a part of it. In fact, were it not for what they as grown men saw her as bestowing on us, they might not have known she was capable of it. By the time they came under her dominion less than four years after their mother's death, Chick and Ralph may have been a little rambunctious in their behavior, or she may have sensed from the first that they resented her, or both. In any case, there was a strong puritanical streak in her, and principle rather than love seems to have guided her in her role as stepmother. I can well imagine it was obvious from the outset, whether because she had the stronger personality or because my grandfather was in some ways a broken man, that things in her house would be done in her way and that the boys could count on very little effective mediation from their father.

Years later, during those Thanksgiving get-togethers, Chick's and Ralph's gruffness with her and their tendency to construe her basically well-meaning questions as invasions of privacy no doubt dated back to their days under her supervision. At that time, young as they were, I suspect they maintained a sense of themselves and their earlier and happier days by resisting her authority as best they could until they were old enough to enlist in the armed forces and gain the confidence and confirmation of their individual identities that they had not received from her. And so much was their attitude to women marked by their experience with Bertha that even my mother had to be careful in her conversation with them lest she be seen as prying. It was as though, having been bullied by one woman, they would never let it happen again. My father and Uncle Jim, who had known their mother the longest, were gentlemen—quiet, polite, and soft-spoken; Chick and Ralph, who had the largest dose of Bertha in their upbringing, ironically, were rougher, less refined. But they were not broken. Although as boys and as grown men there was little love lost between them, they were both, as I came to realize, extremely vulnerable, and their overall "not-to-be-messed-with" exterior may have been assumed in order to keep their feelings, which were always very close to the surface, from showing.

2. Ralph

Of my three Coffin uncles, Ralph was probably the most accessible. If he seemed less distant than his brothers, it was perhaps because he had not been directly marked by the loss of his mother and brother Howard in the way they had. Born premature and weighing less than three pounds—with Millie suffering from the illness she would die of only months later— he was sent off to live and be taken care of by Charles and Nellie Reed on their farm ten miles from Woodstock in

Quechee, Vermont. My grandfather visited him regularly there and often took his other sons along with him, and Ralph was brought to Woodstock to meet his stepmother and spend time with the family. An entry in a diary kept by Haze for a short time in January, 1925 states, "Mrs. Reed with brother Ralph spent the day with us. Ralph is showing all the pep and intelligence displayed by little Howard." It may have been the early impressions from these visits that prompted Ralph to try to hide from his father when he came to see him there on the farm, as the Reeds' granddaughter Nellie recalled him doing. She remembered him as a good-natured, mischievous boy with a love of climbing trees, shinnying up birches to where the branches started and making his way from there up into the heights. There was plenty of love for Ralph in the Reed family, and he was ever grateful for the rough and tumble life they offered him during the years of childhood he spent with them on the farm and at the one-room Hillside School not far away. Had he been allowed to go on living with the Reeds, his life no doubt would have been better, but Hillside School only went up to the eighth grade, and his father's new situation made it possible for him to join the family when he had finished his schooling there. Ralph's life on Lincoln Street was a misery. He was, I imagine, bewildered from the start by his removal from the farm and very much in need of love and understanding, and his new life in his stepmother's house must have seemed like incarceration. Chick, fifteen years old at the time, was from the beginning not happy with Bertha and was, by Ralph's testimony, a bully. In fact, such was Chick's treatment of Ralph from the time of his inclusion in the family there on Lincoln

Street that Ralph bore him resentment all his life and showed no real sadness at the time of his death. And in Bertha he found what he perceived to be a stern, unyielding woman bent on subduing him and teaching him the manners he had not learned from the Reeds.

It has always been easier for me to accept this side of her character than it has for my brother, for we had somewhat different experiences with our grandmother. While it is true that, having no children of her own, she may have discovered belatedly her maternal affection when we were born, it is also true that of the two of us she preferred Howard. At birth, he was the smaller twin, weighing five pounds as opposed to my five pounds and six ounces, and as a child he was somewhat smaller than I and had light blond hair, the color of my father's and Chick's hair when they were boys. Though also thin, I was heavier, and my hair was dark brown. From early on in our lives it seemed that he was a Coffin and I was a Jillson, one of my mother's family. Some of our earliest baby pictures showing the two of us sitting side by side on a couch are an early study in character: I am smiling broadly and leaning affectionately toward Howard, and he is sitting rigidly upright and frowning as if in disapproval of my palsy overtures and as though he'd had enough of crowding in the womb and was resolved to keep his newfound space to himself. The Coffins had much bigger bubbles than the Jillsons: a handshake was as close as you got to the Coffins, while hugs and open demonstrations of affection were the norm among the Jillsons, who, of course, included aunts as well as uncles. I think it no exaggeration to say that Bertha lost her heart to Howard, and she was very protective of him. As it takes no time at all for a child to sense inequities and favoritism, I early began to understand that when Bertha and Howard and I were together, walking up the road to Hartland Hill to look at horses in the meadow or picking berries behind the house, or if she was observing our play at a big washtub full of water on the lawn, I needed to be more than usually careful about getting along with Howard or I'd be in for some stern disapproval if not some downright scolding. Oddly enough, if I suffered no real jealousy of Howard for Grammy Coffin's preference of him, it was mostly because she was not someone I remember trying greatly to please. My feelings were all for my Jillson grandparents, as were my sister's. However, though I don't remember it, I was once told by my mother that I had finally had so much of what I had evidently experienced as Grammy Coffin's discrimination that in some distress I asked Ada Maynes, my parents' best friend, if she would "like me better." I very much regret to say that I had no great affection for Bertha, my step-grandmother. Nor did my sister. She recalls going up to her grandparents on Lincoln Street on Easter to have dinner and to hunt for our Easter baskets, which Grammy would have taken some time to prepare—filling them with chocolates and jelly beans and maple sugar candy and small porcelain figures of rabbits and birds and other animals—and then to hide somewhere inside her house for us to find. Poor Jane, seven years younger than Howard and I, was never able to find her basket and always had to enlist the assistance of Mother after Howard and I had found ours. For Grammy, with no consideration for Jane's feelings, would always have put her basket away in a place that no little girl could possibly have discovered for herself, thus taking all the fun out of it for her and making her Easter Sundays times of confusion and dismay.

It was Bertha's fondness for Howard that made her house on Lincoln Street a different place for him from what it was for me. He evidently experienced none of my eagerness to be free of that house and to go home as soon as the afternoon shadows began to gather and the lamps were turned on. In fact he would sometimes ask my parents' permission to stay overnight there, a desire that is to this day and always will be unimaginable to me. What would anyone do in that house at night? Grammy Coffin was, in all fairness, a generous, resourceful and well-informed woman; though she could not afford to travel, throughout her life she read widely to satisfy her curiosity about geography and history and the mysteries of the natural world. And she was interested in sharing what she had learned. Together, she and Howard would look at pictures and read books. One book in particular, a large tome on the Civil War, with pictures and maps, captured his imagination and was perhaps the beginning of a lifelong interest that led to his becoming a Civil War historian and a leading figure in Civil War battlefield preservation. Then when it got to be bedtime, if such was his wish, they would climb the steep stairs to the attic and sleep in the old bed that remained there from her days as a spinster.

To say the least, Grammy Coffin's stepsons Chick and Ralph in their time with her were strangers to anything like this doting affection. Thus, on rare occasions when they did say anything at all about their life with her and I tried to sympathize with them based on my experience as the less favored grandson, neither one would hear me out. Indeed, they had witnessed and heard enough of Howard's and my privileged status to discredit any complaints I might have about her. However difficult Bertha found her role as stepmother to be, my mother thought there could be no defense for what Ralph suffered under her. Poor Ralph, with his strangely pointed head and his one crossed eye, which required surgery to straighten, evidently could not find favor with her. By the time he came to live at Lincoln Street, my father had found employment in the Woodstock Electric Company in the middle of the village, and eventually my mother worked there for a time. Although my father would never speak of it, my mother remembered Ralph coming into the store to find my father and sobbing there in the presence of someone he felt he could trust to understand what he had been through at her hands until he couldn't take it any more. In those days, before he was married, my father was living there as well with his younger brothers and must have witnessed their difficult relations with their stepmother. And whether or not he ever actively tried to intercede, or appeal to his father to do so, his heart must certainly have gone out to them, for he hated bullying of any sort and was always on the side of the disadvantaged. Somehow Ralph stood it as long as he could, and then, in opposition to her wishes, he quit school and joined the Navy. Her parting words were, he told me, something to the effect that he would never make anything of himself. When he came home after serving his country in World War II on aircraft carriers, he had lost his buddy from Woodstock, Don Paige, who was killed on Okinawa, and he had experienced aboard the Belleau Wood some of the most severe naval combat in the Pacific. He felt lucky to have survived it all, particularly the kamikaze attack east of Leyte in which one of the planes that had been shot down fell on her aft deck, causing fires which set off ammunition. Before the flames were brought under control, 92 men were either dead or missing. At the end of the war, he gave his stepmother a pillow covered in silk with the emblem of the Belleau Wood embroidered on it in gold letters. It was a gift that, he told my mother years later, obviously meant nothing to her; she showed him no gratitude or appreciation for it, though it was, I recall, given a place on the couch in the living room. Not long after his return to Woodstock, he moved to White River Junction, where he went to work for White River Coach Lines and then Vermont Transit Company and where he lived for most of the rest of his life.

Over the years, though Ralph obviously never forgot his troubles at the hands of his stepmother when he was young, he was good to her and his father. When Howard and I were children, before Jane was born, he would sometimes give up a Sunday to take us all out for a ride in his car. This was a special treat for my parents as well as my grandparents, none of whom owned an automobile. This car, a big maroon 1948 Chrysler which he was especially proud of and kept immaculately cleaned and shined up, had wide seats and plenty of leg-room and was big enough for the seven of us. Some of these outings were simple afternoon excursions, but some were longer, and on these we would take a picnic lunch. Sometimes we went to Plymouth State Park and explored the woods, and sometimes we went as far as Fort Ticonderoga on Lake Champlain and Battery Park in Burlington and to Allis State Park in Brookfield and climbed the forest fire tower there to enjoy the spectacular 360-degree view from the top. How much Ralph enjoyed these outings or whether he simply saw them through out of some sense of duty is difficult to say. It seems to me that whenever we were around our Uncle Ralph, my brother and I were two removes from him. That is, he was on the other side of my grandmother and my mother, both of whom were protective of us, so that he never had us to himself, and vice versa. Never, that is, until we were all at the top of Garvin Hill a few miles south of Woodstock, where we had gone to climb the tower for its wide view of Windsor County. When it came time to descend the hill and return to the car, Howard and I wanted to race all the way down through the open pastures and small copses to the car, and Ralph said he would run with us. Whether our wish and his offer prompted from Bertha any sort of interference I don't recall, but we set out racing. At some point after he had gotten out in front of us, we all stopped to catch our breath, and he held out his hands and asked us if we'd like to go faster so as to keep up with him. We eagerly grabbed hold, and he set off. At first, by taking about three steps to every one of his, we were able to stay abreast of him, but as he increased his speed to a dead run, our feet would touch the ground on only every third or fourth step, the pasture and the trees racing by us, and sometimes it felt as if we were flying. We shouted and shrieked in excitement at first, but then in some alarm as his grip tightened and we felt our arms being stretched and the pressure on our shoulders increased. He just kept going as if possessed and driven by something deep within himself; was he running away from something or toward something or somehow both—*away* from all of my grandmother's sheltering love for us and back into his own childhood on the farm to teach us something of the freedom of the rougher side of life, or *toward* some relation with us, the only children to whom he would ever have any blood relation, unsupervised by female advice and governed by his own rules, his own tough love? Howard and I often roughhoused with Poppa, "tussling" he called it; we'd gang up on him in his chair or on the living room rug, but that was affection disguised as aggression, and was no doubt inspired by his loving to hug us. But this was somehow different; there was a kind of violence in it, as though we were being punished for possessing something he had never been shown, or challenged in a sort of rite of passage. As we continued plunging downward, our feet and bare shins brushing the goldenrod and Queen Anne's lace, our arms feeling as though were going to come out of their sockets, the wind sometimes singing in our ears over the pounding of his feet, Howard and I shouted, "stop, stop" and tried to get our feet under us, but he was going far too fast. When we finally reached the car way ahead of the rest of the party, he was winded, and he sort of came to. "There," he panted, "how'd you like that? You boys all right?" We told him we were O.K., and he laughed and said something like "That's the stuff!" as though he was proud of us for passing some sort of initiation. In that run down Garvin Hill, Uncle Ralph had certainly given us something to remember, but what it was I will never fully understand any more than he himself would be likely to do were he alive and reminded of it. If he had not intended it as a sort of toughening up, boot camp exercise, that may be what he had in mind some years later when we were in elementary school and he gave Howard and me boxing gloves for Christmas, a gift which amused my father and irritated my mother. Not long after we put them on and Poppa tied the strings and showed us how to lead with the left hand and to defend ourselves, what started as a civilized, disciplined sparring match soon turned to a flailing, windmill slugfest with both of us in tears. My father threatened to put the gloves away for good if we couldn't show sportsmanlike conduct, and my mother, had Ralph been on hand, might have given him a piece of her mind.

Although Ralph had his share of the Coffin reserve and sense of privacy, he was, in his own way, devoted to the family. He was also, as I discovered later in life, capable of a kind of candor, though it took some work to get him to reveal himself. After the last of his three brothers died in 1983, I think he greatly missed Haze and my father in particular, and he would look in on us from time to time to see how we were getting on. He would park his Chevy Blazer on the side of the street down in front of the house, and we would catch sight of him walking up around the driveway. Since my mother would be annoyed if he showed up around our supper time—after just having had his evening meal at the nearby Wasps Snack Bar—she would caution me: "Oh Lord, now you know he has just eaten at the snack bar, so don't offer him anything; he doesn't need it!" Though he was, to be sure, carrying some extra weight in the midriff, I didn't feel as though I could exclude him. When to

Mother's chagrin I asked him if he would like to join us, he'd always answer, "I don't care," which would further exasperate her because of its indirectness and because she knew it meant "yes." Being an essentially shy man, when he entered, he simply presented himself and said little. In order to avoid what would have been for me, at least, an awkward silence, I usually began the conversation. After Haze's death, he had come into possession of his camp in Barnard, and if it turned out that he was stopping at our house on his way up there to mow the lawns or just to check on the place, I knew that was my invitation to go along with him and help him out if I wanted to. He never would have invited me directly to join him. After we finished the landscaping work up there, we would drive back roads until it grew dark, drinking beer, admiring the landscape, and talking. And he would open up a bit. We knew he had a lady friend, as Howard had happened to see them together once in a restaurant in Lebanon, but we never met her until years later at his funeral in White River. I suppose he had dated various women, but we never knew anything about them, and I doubt they knew anything about us. Though he never married, my mother told me that he had contemplated doing so as a young man. As what little we knew of the story went, she was a White River girl and a Roman Catholic, and, as he admitted to me, his father's anti-Catholic views had been a concern to him, though they may not have been the deciding factor in his decision to stay single. She evidently did not live long, and I think he told me it may have been a heart condition that brought her life to an early end. I was struck by the fact that in this matter religion was of any concern, for it suggested how important it was for this otherwise fiercely independent man to consider the wishes of his father.

In many ways, Ralph was a simple man, but even now what brings him so clearly before the mind's eye is something like the contradictions in his nature. His wartime experiences in the Pacific might have accounted for his rough edges had they not already been pretty firmly in place as a result of his early years on the farm and his youth in the house of his stepmother. Having never known his mother, he had no way of fully realizing, let alone expressing, the softer side of his nature, and no doubt would have denied the existence of any such thing. But it was there, and it was in some recognition of it that I would extend a hand so as to prompt a handshake when I was greeting him, always catching him off guard but receiving a powerful grip when our hands joined. And sometimes I could hear the suggestion of a sort of companionable intimacy when, on our evening drives, he might preface a remark with "You know, Bruce," and my name in direct address meant that I had broken through to something he usually kept pretty well protected. But he had no response to my words of parting when he left me off at the house and I leaned into the car to say, "Thanks; that was a good time. I'll get in touch with you next time I'm in town," except the customary chuckle and the awkward "yeah." Otherwise he kept his feelings pretty well hidden. Where you had to look for them—and this was true of his brothers as well—was in the eyes. On his last day of work before his retirement from Vermont Transit in August of 1985, Howard, Mother, Jane, and I decided to surprise him by going along with him on his final run, a late afternoon round-trip of some 95 miles from White River Junction to Rutland and back. When Ralph saw us standing there at the station waiting to hand him our tickets and board, he predictably showed no emotion, not even surprise. Of the photos we took on this last trip, the best one is of him standing by the open door of the bus with a the hint of a smile on his face, but there is the telltale small wrinkle between the eyes that gets past his defenses and reveals his gratitude. And of the many pictures snapped at the big afternoon retirement party thrown for him in White River by his fellow employees, two in particular show that he was deeply moved by the show of affection from so many friends and well-wishers; his feelings are discernible only to those who know where to look: in the eyes and his brow. Only once do I remember seeing him openly wrestle with his emotions and just barely win the match. It was after my father's funeral in January of 1983 when a number of family members and a few friends had come back to Lincoln Street for coffee and a little something to eat. I had been curiously lethargic and numb since Poppa's death. Our main concern had been my mother and how she would survive without him, but she seemed at that stage to be holding up very well. I had been out in the living room talking with Jane, and I went into the dining room for a sandwich and happened to look across the table at Ralph, who was standing, uncharacteristically in coat and tie, between the door to the kitchen and the china cabinet, facing me. He was holding a plate in his hands. As our eyes met, I at first thought he was chewing something very quickly and energetically, for his lower jaw and chin were moving up and down rapidly. But it was the look of helplessness in his eyes that suddenly made me understand that he was trying with all his might not to break down and sob right then and there. He was too faithful to take himself away and certainly too stoical not to win the battle, but it was, for a time, a close contest. That I recall no such struggle in him after Uncle Jim's funeral leads me to suspect that, beyond his own loss of my father, what was threatening to undo him was his sympathy for my mother and my brother and sister and me.

Ralph looked out for my mother in the eleven years between my father's death and his own, stopping in on her at Lincoln Street, where she lived by herself. He made sure to clear her driveway of snow after every winter storm, and whenever he came to Woodstock, he visited her in the late afternoon or early evening. She would report to me on their times together and tell me how much she enjoyed his company, though she did not see why he sometimes felt it necessary to scratch his back by rubbing it across and then up and down the corner of the kitchen door jamb like some old grizzly bear. She would often be resting on the couch when he arrived; he would sit in Poppa's easy chair, and they would talk about the weather and about us children and our children and then branch out to people in families from the old days, this coded language of affection and understanding being the means of acknowledging so many years of knowing each other. And sometimes when he would fall silent for a few minutes and fail to answer a question of hers, Mother would assume he had just noticed snowflakes beginning to fall outside the west window or had paused to watch a chickadee on the birdfeeder, and she would look over at him and discover his head resting against the back of the chair. He had fallen asleep.

Neither my mother nor I ever spent this kind of time alone with my father's other brothers, and it strikes me that, had it been Haze or Chick instead of Ralph who survived my father, it is doubtful that we'd have come to know them in the same way as we did him. That he was in many ways the most open of them all may be accounted for by his being the only one who did not directly experience the loss of his mother. Though he no doubt regretted all his life—I recall his saying so once— that he had never known her, and though he may have been haunted by the knowledge that his conception was an accident and that his birth had hastened her death, he at least had access to his early years and could recover the people of his first memories simply by visiting them on the farm in Quechee, as he often did. I am tempted to think that his openness and accessibility were original Coffin family characteristics that were fostered there by the Reed family and survived only in him as a result of his not having to bear any share in the grief and anguish that followed Millie's passing from the lives of his father and brothers at such a young age. Ironically, Ralph's nature may have offered the clearest image of his mother's character and of her imprint on the life of her family before the tragedy struck.

I don't remember the last time I saw him. It may have been at the Polka Dot Diner in White River, where I sometimes met him for breakfast. Or it may have been at my nephew Joel's wedding reception in West Lebanon in 1993. At that event, my sister and I sat at the same table as Ralph, and we were both surprised at how heavy he was. He was also having some trouble with his hearing, and he had made so little effort to dress suitably for the event that we wondered if he had, as the saying goes, begun to "let himself go" a little. I knew that he had regular medical check-ups, and since I had no recollection of his ever suffering bad health, I was astonished when my sister phoned me in Connecticut to tell me that Ralph had been found unconscious outside his condominium in Wilder, Vermont. He had apparently suffered a severe heart attack, and it was unlikely that he would recover. On that June night, he must have realized that something was wrong and tried to call 911 and then left the building to seek help. He was taken to the Dartmouth-Hitchcock Medical Center, where he was kept on a life-support system for two days without regaining consciousness. Just two days after receiving this news and two weeks before Ralph's seventy-first birthday, I was alone at Lincoln Street, painting the front bedroom, which had temporarily been emptied of its furniture for that purpose except for one chair. At 4:17 p.m. the phone rang downstairs, and for some reason, out of old habit, I suppose, I picked up the receiver of the dusty old telephone which had been installed in that bedroom in 1958, when we first moved there, not even sure about whether it still worked. It was the hospital calling, and the voice on the line told me that Ralph had died. I thanked the caller, put down the phone, and wandered from room to room upstairs, then went down and stood in the yard for a few moments before returning to the front bedroom, where, I suddenly remembered, my grandmother Coffin had died in 1957 and her sister Lura had died eighteen years later, and where I had just received word that Ralph, the youngest and last of the five Coffin boys, had just passed away. Here I was, by myself, in a room that was reminding me of its own place in the family history, of the lives it had contained, of so much that had happened here. For a short time, the whole house seemed to have a strangely attentive character, and I remembered a passage from Joseph Conrad, "There is a soul in things." The antiquated telephone, assumed to have been disconnected long ago, had just performed what I rightly imagined might be its last service, and the light pouring in through the west windows at that time of the afternoon had a strangely numinous quality that invited listening as well as looking. But there were only the intermittent creakings of the staircases, the mutterings of woodwork issuing from an unusually deep silence and the moments as they succeeded one another—a whole generation was gone—in what I realized was the beginning of my time in the front lines.

Ralph and I would, for a time, have a sort of curious after-life together which would increase the Coffin legacy of the unspoken and enhance my memories and understanding of him. His will appointed his two nephews and his niece as his heirs, and Howard and I were designated his executors. After his bank accounts and insurance policies were located and all his papers were gone through, it fell to me to track down and to dispose of his belongings throughout the summer of 1994 and for some time afterwards. Because his condo had so little storage space, he had parked and stored many of his posses-sions with his friends all over White River Junction and the neighboring town of Wilder. There were two handguns and several rifles to be appraised and sold as well as his Chevy Blazer, his ride-around tractor mower, some trailers, hand lawn mowers, wheelbarrows, ladders, chainsaws, and tools and appliances of all sorts. My task required interviewing a number of people at the bus station who could refer me to other people who either had some of his things in their possession or knew of their whereabouts, and then making appointments to visit these people. Sometimes I met some pretty stiff resistance, inspired in part by loyalty. On the telephone with the man who, I had been told, was keeping Ralph's tractor mower in his garage, I explained who I was and why I was calling, only to be told, "I don't know who you are, Mister, but I'll tell you one thing: you'd better be able to prove you're a close relation of Ralph's because that man was like a father to me, and nobody, and I mean nobody, is going to lay a hand on his things unless they have some damned good right to them!" It was with some trepidation, therefore, that a few days later I approached a small house on a street near the bus station, well armed with a bill of sale and the serial number of the tractor mower and plenty of personal identification. Oddly enough, the man I was seeking answered the door with tears streaming down his face and was joined by his mother, who was also weeping. Before I could begin feeling guilty for dispossessing them, I was asked into the kitchen and understood the cause—the two of them were boiling and canning pickled onions—and I began to feel my own eyes starting to water. Once I had established my own identity and legitimacy, he was less suspicious, even a little more friendly, than he had been on the phone. He told me that Ralph had lived near him and his mother, and in the absence of a father, had kept an eye on him, often stopping by to give him rides to school in bad weather, and he wasn't going to let anyone desecrate or dishonor Ralph or his belongings. He wasn't going to allow anyone to make off with anything which, I suspected, he might have gotten away with keeping had I been less vigilant.

The rest of my encounters as Ralph's executor were less dramatic and usually took place on summer evenings when people were home from work. I'd leave Woodstock in the late afternoon in his Chevy Blazer and drive the fourteen miles to White River Junction, which was even more quiet at that time of day than it had been on those mornings when I had gone there to meet him for breakfast. I'd park in front of The Polka Dot and go in for supper at the same tables we used to occupy. My first time there alone, I noticed a certain hushed curiosity when a waitress coming on duty stepped in the door and surveyed the clientele somewhat warily before taking her place behind the counter. Then it struck me, and when I went to pay my bill, I explained to her and the owner of the diner who I was and what Ralph's car with its familiar license plate— 5510—that he had had for years was doing out next to the curb. Grateful for my having solved that small mystery, they responded as people always did at the mention of Ralph's name—with a smile that acknowledged he was something of a character, and a wistful assurance that he was "a good man" or "a great guy" and that they "missed him" after so many years of his taking his meals there. Experiences of this sort, in which, first of all, I had to prove my relation to him and then to explain that, his car to the contrary, he was, indeed, no longer to be seen in his town among his people, began to give me a sense of somehow *being* Ralph. My evening trips from Lincoln Street to White River Junction were, after all, the ones he had made after visiting us, and my solitary stops at The Polka Dot were his. I was a stranger in this town, but then again, though Ralph was recognized here, I was sure he kept much of his life to himself and there was much about him, his early years in particular, that remained unknown even to those who knew him best. As my ongoing duties took me to more places and brought me in touch with more of his friends, I'd find myself in less of a hurry to transact business and return to Woodstock. The Estabrooks had given Ralph some storage space at their home in the south end fronting the railroad tracks. Bob Estabrook had been a driver with Vermont Transit for years until a weak heart forced him into retirement, and he and his wife were usually to be found at home, enjoying the summer air on their front porch when I stopped by. After recovering from the shock of seeing Ralph's blazer entering their driveway, they invited me in for a chat before leading me out to the garage to gather up another load of his tools. I never did find or dispense with all of his belongings and gave much of the stuff away or sold it at fair prices to his friends, and as the summer wore on, my excursions as executor became more social than business occasions. And whether it was because I was retracing Ralph's footsteps and mingling with his friends and driving his car and generally living these evenings in his world, or because I began to see this world in a new way or both, White River Junction, which is in many ways the antithesis of Woodstock and had always seemed like an alien place, began to feel like home, or at least a place that could be home. Wasn't this discovery too a re-enactment of Ralph's experience? By the time of his last years there, White River had long since ceased to be a busy and prosperous railway center and in spite of ongoing attempts to resuscitate itself, had come to look something like a ghost town. Those evenings after I had paid my visits, I took to wandering around—with Ralph's spirit as good company—past empty storefronts that stretched down the main streets, and large buildings once housing banks and a post office, now closed and deserted, the late sun glinting off the dusty windows of their vacant offices and empty rooms. The large brick Tip Top Bakery had long since dismissed its shift workers and closed its doors. Down along the railroad tracks, abandoned tankers, freight and passenger cars had been shunted off on rusting, weed-strewn rails. The rail service, which was limited to two daily Amtrak arrivals and departures, one in the middle of the night, was now more a matter of history than of commerce and transportation. The Coolidge Hotel on the main square, still miraculously open for business, beckoned from its grand lobby with its comfortable old chairs to anyone looking for the quietest place on earth. Though Ralph might have regretted the marginalization of the busy industrial town with its traffic and its nightlife that had attracted him as a young man, he might also have come to favor the quiet that had set in there later in his life. And I thought it quite likely that he had found solace in the assurance that White River Junction, in spite of its commercial depression and economic woes, had kept its soul as it grew old with him. It would be here and not in Woodstock that I would continue to sense his presence.

3. Chick

As the youngest of the Coffin boys to remember his mother and the closest in age to his brother Howard, Chick may have been the most lost of them all during and after the autumn of 1923. And he may have resented most deeply the differences between his mother and his stepmother. I don't know very much about his early life, that is, from the time of his birth in 1911 until he came to live at Lincoln Street when he was fifteen. He eventually graduated from high school in 1931 and occupied himself in some way for a decade before joining the Marines. Neither he nor Ralph would say much about those years. He was less sympathetic and more self-serving than his brothers. But under his gruff and sometimes hostile-seeming mien, was, it seems to me, a great vulnerability, and in some ways his emotions may have been so close to the surface that he needed to be perpetually on guard lest he be ambushed by them. From the time he returned to Woodstock after the war, battle-scarred from combat in the Pacific island jungles—he was four days lost behind enemy lines on Guadalcanal and was wounded in the hip by shrapnel—he was not often seen at Lincoln Street. For some years he worked factory jobs in Windsor and Springfield, Vermont, then surprised everyone by marrying a woman many years older than he and settling temporarily in Woodstock in an apartment on River Street. His wife, Violet Powers, had been married and divorced twice before she met Chick, and she had two grownup daughters by her first marriage. She was also the heir of two wealthy, aging maiden aunts living in Maine, and the prospect of a sizeable inheritance was for Chick no doubt one of the principal inducements to marriage. Beyond these prospects and a mutual interest in the bottle, it is difficult to see what, if anything, Chick and Vi had in common. She had been raised in a large house on Elm Street and had manners and was, in her way, quite stylish in dress and appearance, but she had a tendency to become silly and tiresome when she had had a few drinks, which was fairly often. Chick too was a drinker. For years a bent iron post and railing on the south side of the Green in Woodstock marked the place where, after emerging from a long soak in the Woodstock Inn's Pine Room late one night, he had failed to turn his yellow Willis Jeep truck onto Route 4 and drove instead straight across the street into the park fence. It was no doubt this event and others like it which, when Chick's name comes up, accounts for the reaction of the dwindling number of people who remember my father's brothers. I have grown accustomed to hearing something like, "Let's see, there was Haze, who worked in the post office, and Ralph, who drove the bus," and after a pause, I'd supply the name of Chick, which would usually provoke a smile and a shake of the head, followed by something like, "he was a piece of work" or "he liked to raise a little hell." I don't know why he was nineteen years old when he graduated from high school, but I have always assumed he must have been held back at some point, most likely for lack of application. A bit of ribaldry

scrawled in one of his school books found in the attic at
Lincoln Street suggests he had things other than his studies on
his mind: "Here's to the maid of seventeen,/Oh are your
evenings free?/I'll take you off to Taftsville,/What'll you take
off for me?"

Bertha disapproved of his marriage and had little use for
Vi, though the two of them got along on the rare occasion
when they were in each other's company. Vi had enough class
to keep her real feelings for Bertha from showing, and was
always polite; and Bertha, who was very much against drinking,
was coldly civil to her. My parents too had little patience for Vi
though they knew she was basically goodhearted and that her
life with Chick, which she must have entered with her eyes
open (though perhaps a little blurred), was probably not an
easy one. Years after Bertha died and they moved first to
Connecticut and then to Maine to be nearer to her inconsider-
ately long-lived aunts, their visits to Woodstock were infre-
quent. But once a year or so, often around Alumni Day in June,
they would show up and check in for a few days' stay at the
Shiretown Inn or, after they had come into their inheritance,
the Woodstock Inn. If my parents could avoid them, which
was difficult because they tended to show up at Lincoln Street
unannounced, they would, but usually they just steeled themselves for the visit and got through it somehow without
showing their boredom or irritation. Right from the moment
when my mother answered the door and affected surprise and
delight, things were at least somewhat awkward. Chick, a
Coffin, was reserved and undemonstrative; Violet, on the other
hand, was loud and tiresomely effusive and was inclined,

especially if she had taken a nip or two before arriving, to dispense hugs, something that was so against my father's nature that he would stand frozen when he saw anyone closing in on him. The four of them would sit in the living room, and Mother would sometimes serve coffee. Had Chick been there by himself, I believe the conversation would have found a natural, slow-paced rhythm of inquiry and comment about us children and about Uncle Jim or Ralph and other Woodstock people he and my parents knew in common. However, with Violet there, things were otherwise: she assumed most of the burden of talk, was evidently uncomfortable with pauses, and tended to ramble on about people and things unknown and of little interest to anyone but herself, and to draw out her anecdotes with a good deal of the "I-said-to-her . . ." and "she-said-to-me . . ." sort of detail that shows very little concern for the listener and can try anyone's patience. Mother would do her best to feign interest, as would my father, though he wasn't very good at it. During these monologues, Chick would be sitting there in Poppa's easy chair, paunchy and immobile, looking straight ahead of him out of his heavily lidded eyes with a glowering expression until he had heard enough, and then he would startle everyone by turning his head in Vi's direction and sonorously declaring, "You talk too much." If that quieted her down, it was usually not for long, and once she was wound up again, Chick, taking advantage of her impaired hearing, would tell my parents out of the side of his mouth that one of these days he was "going to loosen some boards on the cellar stairs."

Once Howard and I were in college, we didn't mind assuming some of the responsibility for receiving and entertaining them on their visits to Woodstock. On at least two occasions, they turned up at Lincoln Street when one of our parties was in full swing. My parents joined us in these parties, which were beery and noisy, with the record player blasting folk music when there was no one who happened to have a guitar. With everyone in high spirits, Chick and Vi would be greeted by Howard and me and our friends as honored guests. Vi, no doubt feeling young again and in her element among so many young men, would become amorous and silly, patting our cheeks and shuffling a few dance steps to some song she'd begin to sing before breaking into giggles. And Chick I can still see, just as he was, standing in the crowded, cigarette-smoke-filled kitchen, a beer in his hand, his wary eyes, as always, puddling up slightly from the personal attention he was receiving from young people, and wearing a kind of knowing little smile suggesting he was greatly enjoying the thought of Bertha turning over in her grave at the sight of her family home put to such uses. It might well have seemed strange to him to see the Metcalf house as a place of revelry and happiness for two generations of Coffins, parents and children alike. Sometimes when Howard and I heard that he and Vi were in town, we would join them at the Woodstock Inn's Pine room or in their hotel room. Once we arrived too early and witnessed something of the downside of their boozy evenings with Vi staggering around and complaining that Chick wouldn't let her have another drink and charging him with not really loving her, until Chick told her to shut up and go to bed.

Then when she was safely asleep, he removed the whisky bottle from the water tank in the back of the toilet where he had hidden it, and poured the three of us a couple of shots, and we talked to him about old Woodstock and about his experiences in the war, but never about his childhood.

Chick and Vi had to wait a long time for their money. Both of her aunts lived into and beyond their nineties before passing on sometime in the 1970s and leaving them well over half a million dollars. My parents learned of their inheritance from them during one of their visits to Woodstock from their home in Kennebunk, Maine. To Mother and Poppa, who had never had much money and knew that wealth of any sort had little to do with happiness, Chick and Vi's excitement over receiving a sum in excess of what they had long anticipated was understandable but also pathetic in that money seemed to be about all they had. As Vi was going on about what their new fortune would mean to them, including a much needed new car, Chick turned to my parents and muttered, "I'm going to buy her a Jaguar," suggesting, perhaps, not so much that it would be a relief to be rid of her in a high-speed traffic accident as that he was in sympathy with any boredom my parents might be suffering from her endless nattering.

By the time Chick was diagnosed with emphysema in the late 70s, Vi had become frail and was living in a nursing home near their house in Maine. He eventually died in 1982 in his easy chair and was found there by the cleaning lady the next morning. He had never been one for close family ties. Though he did stop to see us in Woodstock and usually at least tried to see Haze as well, he never, as far as I know, went out of his

way to find Ralph. Whatever Ralph's feelings may have been—
and I suspect he was at least somewhat bothered at having
been excluded—he would let it be known that he had no desire
to see Chick. I have always suspected that in addition to the
bullying Ralph suffered at Chick's hands, shame had a great
deal to do with their uneasiness around each other. In the
Metcalf house under their stepmother's supervision, they had
seen each other defenseless and humiliated, and I don't think
either one of them ever got beyond the discomfiting sense of
the other as witness. Of all of them, Chick had the most
difficulty in reaching out to people, and it is unlikely that his
marriage really brought him out of himself. His brothers agreed
that he had always served number one at the expense of
anyone else, and I can well remember their sense of outrage
when it reached their ears that on one of his visits to town he
had taken his father out for an afternoon ride when he had had
too many drinks to be driving. Vi outlived him by a few years,
and her money went to her daughters. The last time I saw
Chick was at their home in Kennebunk, about a year before his
death. Maria and I and the children were on our way home
from Deer Island, Maine in the summer of 1981, and we found
their address in the phone directory and stopped by. Chick was
by himself and was surprised to see us, as he rarely received
visits from family. My brother, some years before, had been the
only one ever to spend time with him there at his home. By
then he was heavier than I had ever seen him and was wearing
glasses with thick lenses. We stayed and talked for an hour or
so, and as we left and were saying goodbye out on the lawn, we
decided to take a picture of three generations of Coffins. In the

small Polaroid color photo that Maria snapped, I am standing on one side of Chick and holding two-year-old Jonathan; and Lizzie, then seven years old, is standing on the other. It seems ironic to me that the earliest and the last pictures we have of him are family photos. Among the heirlooms found at Lincoln Street is a photo of a stout, brown-haired woman and a group of twenty or so children—some of them infants and toddlers, others perhaps ten or twelve years old—the youngest seated in the front and the oldest kneeling or standing behind them. The woman is Chick's mother, Mildred, and she is looking down at him seated in the front row at her feet and holding his little brother Howard in his lap with his left arm draped around him. As Chick would lose both of them before he was twelve, the photo seems to catch him happy and secure in the early years of a life in which family would have only a small part, no doubt because of those early losses and what followed them in his youth and early manhood with his father and stepmother on Lincoln Street.

4. Haze (Uncle Jim)

My father and his bothers were men of deep feeling, though it sometimes took a trained eye to spot it. The reserve they shared, their sense of privacy, was most likely not the inheritance of the family situation depicted in the letters of 1922-23, but rather of the events that brought that world to a close and of the situation that followed. They were all in one way or another survivors, reluctant to revisit what they had been through and what they had lost. Though they did not see a great deal of each other in their adult lives, I think they cared deeply for each other in some area of their personalities that was not to be opened or outwardly expressed. My mother once related to me a scene she thought typical of the Coffins. She and my father had stopped at the supermarket in Woodstock, and she noticed Uncle Jim coming out of the market just as my father was approaching the door. They did not acknowledge one another. Uncle Jim walked to his car to deposit his groceries and then walked back to a spot near the entryway and lit a cigarette and stood looking out over the parking lot. When my father emerged from the store, he put down his bag of groceries and stood beside his brother and lit a cigarette. Neither of them looked at the other, and it was a short while before she could see their mouths moving. They stood so for a few moments and then separated, going their own ways, and leaving my mother to understand that, appearances to the contrary, she had just witnessed a friendly get-together. That anecdote was typical of her affection for my father, but it was also an expression of wonder at the Coffin family distance and restraint. And it was reassuring to me to know that she saw them in the same way I did. Around them all, in slightly differing degrees, the best I could do was to accept what seemed to be their tacit invitation to be as self-possessed as they were. In their company, feeling was something that needed to be left at the door, and enthusiasm was to be well-tempered so as not to embarrass them and myself by seeming effusive. Uncle Jim had the same quiet and dignified presence as my father, the same calm and reserved manner. In their way, they were close, though that seems an odd word to use to describe any of the Coffins. They looked and dressed alike—as town men; that is, they eschewed plaid and denim of any sort and wore slacks or khakis with open-necked, striped or white shirts and lace-up leather shoes. Since they were only three years apart, they had had some of the same friends in high school and afterwards. One photo that has come down to me captures a group of them in 1938, two years before my parents were married. My father, Uncle Jim, and two of their friends are arranged beside a four-door black Ford sedan from the mid-30s, which appears to be parked in a field on top of a hill. Standing at an oblique angle to the camera, Uncle Jim seems to be saying something, either to Dick Eaton, whose back is to the camera as he bends over the running board to open a bottle, or to the two men in the foreground, Gene Roy and my father. Gene is drinking out of a large bottle he has tilted straight up, and my father, facing him, is laughing, perhaps at the size of the swigs being taken or at a characteristically wry remark of Uncle Jim's or both. For this outing in the country, all four of them are dressed in white shirts and dark-colored dress pants as though they had just shed sports coats or suit jackets and ties. They also got together for Ivy League football games in the late 20s and 30s, usually at Dartmouth, but sometimes traveling as far as Cambridge and New Haven for games at Harvard and Yale. As I heard it later in life when my father and I, in the manner of those old days, drank beer together, these were times for roadhouses along the way, both going and coming back, and for pocket flasks during the games. A photo of Uncle Jim in hat, topcoat, and tie always brings to mind a story he told me about one of those outings. At the end of a game at Harvard Stadium in which Dartmouth had trounced the Crimson, he and my father and their mates, no doubt well fortified with whiskey against the cold, joined the mob attempting to tear down the goalposts. They made their way down out of the stands and into the melee of Dartmouth fans on the attack and Harvard fans on the defense. Pushing into the middle of the fracas, Uncle Jim was suddenly confronted by an enormous opponent, who, before he could square off or put up his dukes to defend himself, launched a powerful uppercut that narrowly missed his chin, but caught his hat brim with such force as to lift his hat clean off his head and send it sailing, something that made him quickly decide that discretion is the better part of valor, pick up his hat, and retreat. In his words, some forty years after the event, "If that guy had connected, I'd still be lying there." Back in their heyday, they needed to keep Bertha (who did not share Millie's tolerance of alcohol) from knowing what they were up to. Once, while Uncle Jim was still living at home, she found his store of bottled home brew hidden in the bottom cupboards of the root cellar and dumped it all out in back of the house and disposed of the bottles, making it necessary for him, from then on, to hide his supply in the barn of a neighbor and high school classmate, Inez Watkins, at 25 Lincoln Street, where he was welcome to go and imbibe and play cards in the evening.

Though a couple of drinks could get Uncle Jim to talking about the old days, he (like his brothers) never spoke about his first home and the events that brought it to an end when he was nineteen. Still, he was devoted, in his way, to his father and stepmother and was their mainstay as they grew older. After living in various apartments in Woodstock as a young man, he moved back to Lincoln Street for a time during Bertha's last years and was instrumental in the upkeep of the house and the maintenance of the property there. He kept the lawns mowed and the driveway cleared of snow, and for a time he cultivated a large vegetable garden for them down on the side lawn. He helped them keep abreast of the times by buying for them a television set, a pressure cooker, and other such amenities. My grandparents did not own a car, and neither of them could drive, and although they had their groceries delivered, it would have been difficult for them to get out and about without his assistance. Uncle Jim was a thoughtful and good-hearted man, and my family certainly benefitted from his consideration and generosity. Had it not been for his offering my parents the loan of his jeep when we were children, we would not have been able to enjoy our wonderful one-day summer trips to Lake Morey, in Fairlee, Vermont. And every year at Christmas in those days, he went to considerable expense to buy Howard and me and Jane gifts which my parents would not have been able to afford. On Christmas afternoon, long after my grand-parents had departed, he used to stop by our apartment on Pleasant Street with these presents. I can still remember exactly my great excitement when Howard and I unwrapped the ski outfits—gray ski pants and black nylon windbreakers—that were much in fashion then, and Jane remembers how much she loved the small dressing table and chair and the hand-carved jewelry box with the oriental motifs which he gave her, somehow or other having understood what would be the perfect gift for a girl of her age. He also used to give us season tickets to Dartmouth athletic events and saw to it that we had the use of his jeep so that we could attend them. A sense of family never deserted him. Besides us, he had a sort of surrogate family with whom he spent a great deal of time. A close hunting and fishing friend of his, Jack Pearsons, drowned in 1960 while fishing by himself and left behind his wife Lucille and two children. After that, Uncle Jim took up with Lucille and spent much of his time at her house on Maple Street, becoming a sort of uncle to the children and, eventually, a surrogate grandfather to those children's children.

Uncle Jim's generosity and his understanding of our needs showed itself in a situation which might have inspired resentment in a man of smaller moral stature. When Bertha died and the contents of her will revealed that she had left her entire estate to her grandchildren—the house to Howard and me and a sum of money to both of us and to Jane—Uncle Jim admitted to my father and mother that he was surprised to have been excluded. But he also said he could understand her wishes since the house was for a family, and it would mean that the five of us would no longer be squeezed into our small apartment with only two bedrooms. He had, he assured them, adequate means to find himself a place in town that would suit him until he could carry out his dream of building his own small house in Gray Camp in Barnard, eight miles from Woodstock. After he vacated the house for us in the fall of 1958 and moved into a very comfortable small apartment in the center of the village, he often came by to visit us. On the first of these visits sometime after we had settled in and my father had stripped the downstairs woodwork of its dark varnish and coated it with a much lighter one and I had painted the sash white and made some other small improvements, he was impressed and said how much more homey and welcoming it looked than it had when he had lived there with his father and stepmother. Even after he had retired from the postal service in 1959 and moved to his new house in Barnard, he regularly stopped in to see my parents, and when I was home from college or from wherever I was living after that, my father would be sure to take me up to his house to see him. When he came to see us, he and my father would sit at the small kitchen table, and it would be up to mother to begin the conversation by inquiring about his life in Barnard. And whether he was answering a question or volunteering information, the rhythm would be the same, reminding me of Bob and Ray's famous "Slow Talkers of America" routine: he would begin to speak, then leave off to stir his coffee, a number of expressions crossing his face as he thought about his subject. Then he'd move his head down obliquely once or twice in a gesture between a shake and a nod, somehow both emphatic and conjectural. Then he would add a few words before taking a first sip of coffee from his spoon. Sometimes it would be difficult for me to know whether his silences meant that he had made his point or whether he was simply gathering his thoughts or letting the scene he was considering play itself out in his mind's eye before continuing. After staying with us for an hour or so, he would be on his way. These times with us included a stop on Christmas afternoon, as in the old days when we were children, and my father would have a little something for him in the way of holiday cheer, usually a fifth of Chivas Regal. For my father, who, at most, liked a few beers on Saturday night, and for Uncle Jim, who never liked beer, and—his bibulous days long behind him—seldom drank hard liquor, this was the scotch of choice. Mother and I and Howard and Jane always enjoyed these times for the way they brought the two brothers a little out of themselves. I suppose the one or two drinks they took were a kind of salute to the old days of their escapades during and after Prohibition. Just as with my father, drink made Uncle Jim lighter, more gregarious and inclined to laughter, and it brought out the comical side that I had heard so much about from his old high school classmates and other members of his generation. Though it never speeded up his conversation, it tended to inspire wry comments somewhat in the W. C. Fields mode. I remember him on our front porch at the surprise party we held for my father on the afternoon of his 60th birthday. At that time there was a great deal of road construction in progress on our section of Lincoln Street. Some underground pipes were being replaced, and from a point below our house all the way to the top of the hill, deep trenches scarred both sides of the road, which were piled high with mountains of dirt and large rocks. Uncle Jim scanned the entire project, took a sip of scotch, and said, "I see you've been doing a little hoeing, Wally." He rarely told jokes, but I do remember one: A traveling salesman was driving through he countryside with an upset stomach, frantically looking for some place where he might relieve himself. As his distress became more and more dire, he finally spotted a farmhouse and noticed the farmer standing outside. Wheeling his car into the yard and rapidly explaining his situation, he was pointed in the direction of the outhouse and began hot-footing it across the lawn, only to become tangled up in the clothesline, lose his footing, and fall down and have a dreadful accident in his trousers as he struck the ground. When the farmer caught up with him and expressed his regret for what had happened, the salesman replied, "That's all right, I wouldn't have made it anyway."

Uncle Jim's life in the country greatly suited him. Unlike the other members of Gray Camp, who made use of their camps during deer season and sometime on weekends in the summer months, he lived in his house year around, and the corporation was happy to have someone there who could watch over the many acres of property and feed the fish in the stocked pond. His place, which sat at the end of a long, gently ascending driveway just beyond a copse of white birches, was the best of the lot. With an International Scout he bought as an all-purpose vehicle, he cleared the land of trees and stumps and rocks so he could have a lawn that surrounded both the house and the combination woodshed and tool shed, and bordered both sides of the driveway. There by himself, he led a largely self-sufficient life in retirement, plowing his own snow in winter, cutting some of his own wood for his stone fireplace, and coming into town once a week or so to stock up on items he couldn't buy at the Barnard General Store and to keep in touch with us and the Pearsons family. When my father and I visited him there, we found his pine-paneled house stocked with books about the natural world. Having inherited something of his mother and father's love of animals, he often reported on birds that had appeared on his feeder or deer and bear that had wandered across his lawn. Sometimes, in his wanderings in the surrounding forest or his visits to the pond, he would catch sight of a bobcat or an otter. Even before he had taken up residence at Gray Camp, he had hunted deer for many years, but was the only hunter any of us had ever heard of who had never brought one in. In answer to the ribbing he took from his fellow hunters for what he referred to as his bad luck, he'd mention spotting one but of not being sure it was a buck, and would speak about accidentally startling one before he could raise his rifle. I suspect that in the days before he had his own house and went into camp with the other men, it was the ritual of hunting season that intrigued Uncle Jim—the card-playing at night, the beer, the jokes, the hunting stories, the whisky against the cold, the big breakfasts before dawn—and not the actual stalking to kill. For, like my father, who never hunted or owned a gun, he had, I think, too much love and respect for any of the beautiful creatures with whom he shared the land to think of gunning them down, though he never offered that as a reason for his failure to shoot a deer.

To the end of his days, he stayed true to the life he had created for himself there in the wilderness. When, in his early 70s, he, like Chick, found out that he had emphysema, he made up his mind that he would not go into a hospital or any sort of treatment center. Instead, he would weather the disease as best he could, and, when the time came, he would die there at his home in Gray Camp. As the disease progressed, he never complained. He continued to stop at Lincoln Street from time to time to see my parents, but his visits began to take place later in the day, in the afternoon rather than at midmorning. The reason, as my mother later learned from him, was that as the supply of oxygen to his brain diminished, it would take him a good part of the morning there at his small kitchen table over his coffee to remember who he was and where he was. However frightening those struggles to recover his identity and his whereabouts must have been, he evidently preferred them to medication and hospital visits and oxygen tanks. Finally, there was a stretch of days in the early winter of 1978 when no one had seen him, and my cousin Jim Jillson (who was married to Lucille Pearsons' daughter), fearing the worst, made his way over the snowy roads up to Gray Camp, pulled into Uncle Jim's yard next to his snow-covered Scout, stepped out of his truck, and knew instantly that he had died and was inside the house. Unfortunately, it fell to him to enter the overheated house and find the already decomposing body in bed under an electric blanket.

Uncle Jim died pretty much as he had chosen to live, in his own way, alone, in the place he had made for himself, without being a burden to anyone. Whenever I wonder, as I often have, whether he had ever considered renouncing his bachelor life for the one my father had chosen, I recall something I once heard from my mother: she remembered his telling her that he might have married and started his own family had it not been for Bertha. Although he was nineteen years old when his mother died and twenty three years old when his father remarried, and thus did not come under his stepmother's influence early, as did Chick and Ralph, his years living with her and his father no doubt in some way colored his impressions of marriage per se and perhaps darkened his image of women as wives. Though Bertha was, I believe, generally grateful to Uncle Jim for his generosity and for what he contributed to the upkeep of the house while he lived there, I remember his informing my mother that in spite of his best efforts, he did not always succeed in pleasing her. When she was in the hospital being treated for cancer a year or so before her death, he decided to surprise her by undertaking some improvements to the house. He had the kitchen painted, and he replaced the old claw-footed tub in the upstairs bathroom, which he also had painted, with a more modern tub and shower that sat flat on the floor and was easier to get in and out of. When she returned from the hospital, she was not pleased with his efforts and she lost no time in letting him know it. Still, the three of them managed to live in the house on Lincoln Street in harmony, and she did her best to manage the household until her illness caused her to take to her bed. Then, with a great deal of help from my mother, my grandfather and Uncle Jim did what they could to care for her in her last days. I know my grandfather was deeply grateful for all she had done for him and the family in their thirty years together. And I know that Uncle Jim, who, of the four boys, knew her best, respected her devotion to his father. Though at times he no doubt found her formidable and trying, it was obvious that, in his way, he still held her in high regard.

5. Wallace (My Father)

However much Haze, Chick and Ralph had succeeded in putting behind them a painfully bright vision of their childhood home, like something glimpsed in gathering darkness through the wrong end of a telescope, they seemed to have thought it would be folly for them to trust marriage and a family of their own as a way to recover and perpetuate that early happiness. That trust and recovery were precisely what set my father apart from his brothers. According to my mother, he told her that she was like his mother in character. Wally Coffin and Arlene Jillson met in the 1930s when she went to work for The Woodstock Electric Company, where my father had been employed for a number of years. About their courtship I know very little. That they cared for each other deeply and had done so since they first began going out together was apparent to anyone who knew them, including Bea Johnson, a native of Woodstock who lived in the village all her life. In her early 90s, she told Jane that she remembered seeing them when she was a waitress in the Woodstock Hotel on Central Street in the days before they were married. This place, which was known locally as The Tavern, had a sort of romantic, night club ambiance with its dark blue leather booths and highly polished table tops, and its lights turned down low; and of all the places in Woodstock affordable to the working class, it was the one for stepping out. Bea recalled the two of them coming in on a snowy winter night and selecting a booth, and she described to Jane in precise detail how my father helped my mother off with

her coat and then her boots, which he carried over and placed
next to a radiator to dry. And the reason she remembered it so
clearly, she said, as though it were yesterday, was that it was
obvious that he adored her. I'm sure he did, and it seems just
right to me that the strength of that feeling was discernible in a
gesture of that sort—what he was so careful to do with her
boots—rather than in any open displays of affection, something which he found embarrassing. When he used to take
Howard and me to the movies at the Town Hall theatre on
Sunday nights, he would grow restive and impatient during the
romantic scenes, sometimes even waving his hand at the screen
in a contemptuously dismissive gesture as though to make the
hugging and kissing go away. He and my mother used to tell us
about the great times they had when they went out dancing. It
was the era of the big bands, and with friends—Dick and
Marian Eaton, Gene and Nancy Roy, Uncle Jim and Alice
Leonard and others—they went to the Top Hat in Windsor
and especially the Opera House in Claremont, New Hampshire
to hear Glenn Miller and the Tommy and Jimmy Dorsey bands
and other great dance orchestras of the day. But I never
actually saw them together on the dance floor until I was in
high school, and I was amazed: they were touching each other!
It was not at all that they were dancing cheek to cheek (heaven
forbid!) but it was simply their joined hands, with his arm
around her waist and hers on his shoulder. I might have felt as
though I had caught them in a very private moment had not
their postures been serving some purpose and serving it very
well, for they were wonderful dancers. Instead of "sawing
logs"— our junior high school dance instructors' contemptu-

ous expression for the way we neophytes, boys and girls, used to sway our upper bodies back and forth to the music when we were slow dancing—my mother and father, like the best of their generation, stood straight and, perfectly synchronized, simply glided across the floor. They were clearly enjoying themselves, though my father, perhaps just a little embarrassed, always had a way of suggesting that dancing had been my mother's idea. And, as she told me in some amusement, once out there, if and when they happened to pass Uncle Jim and his partner two-stepping with the best of them, either my father or Uncle Jim or both in unison would ask each other, "How are you standing it?" as though to rescue some of their dignity by assuring each other that men danced only at the request of women.

I suppose what the days of their courtship must have been like was glimpsed by us only a few times, back when we were children. Once in a while they would go out with friends for the evening and leave "Aunt" Ada Maynes from next door or my mother's youngest sister, Anna, to stay with us. But they would always come back to our apartment for a drink—and to check on us—before moving on to another spot. Howard and I would be allowed to join them briefly before returning to our bunk beds and slyly opening the warm air register in the floor to listen to their laughter, and, if possible, to catch a glimpse of them as well. Perhaps it was the rarity of these events that has made them into indelible images of that generation in its prime: my father and Uncle Jim, having just come in with their top coats on, clean shaven, their hair slicked back; my mother and Alice Leonard in their best dresses, with hair freshly permed, the eyes of them all shining with good humor, no doubt partly inspired by a few drinks, and the air scented with perfume in that small apartment, which suddenly looked both cozier and brighter in the lamplight. This was a nocturnal life apart from us children, which carried with it a radiance of the lighted interiors of restaurants and dance floors and apartments and the mystery of the places they had come from, like the magnificent old Woodstock Inn, and the world of streetlights and hours on the clock we had seldom seen. And it is curiously inseparable from the songs my mother used to sing as she was going about her household chores, washing the dishes or cleaning the windows or sweeping the floor or wringing out clothes in the old washing machine: "My Dreams Are Getting Better All the Time" or "Mairzy Doats" or the great aria "I Dreamt I Dwelt in Marble Halls" from Michael W. Balphe's opera *The Bohemian Girl,* and the two Irving Berlin songs she told me my father loved: "The Girl That I Marry" and "In Your Easter Bonnet," snatches of which, when they drift back to me across the years, carry with them her ubiquitous presence along with the spirit of post-World War II optimism and the faces of so many Woodstock people born in the first two decades of the twentieth century that it seems impossible they have all disappeared.

They were such devoted parents that they were hardly away from us at all. That is not to say that, initially, my father was in favor of having a family. In fact, such were the memories of his mother's accidental and fatal last pregnancy and of his little brother's death, that when he first heard his wife was expecting, he would not speak to her for a time, and he must have

worried terribly throughout the months of waiting for their
first baby. Clearly, it was just as well he didn't know there
would be two of us. But from the time we were born, he could
not have been a more loving or attentive father. Nevertheless,
seven years later his reaction was somewhat the same: though
he was less upset than he had been the first time, he was not
pleased at first when he heard my mother was once again
pregnant, perhaps because he thought that this would certainly
be tempting the fates or would awaken the nemesis that
shadowed his earlier family. Yet, from the time my sister was
born, on Howard's and my seventh birthday, she was someone
very special to him. I can still see him putting down the
telephone after hearing the news from the hospital and saying
in a voice muffled by emotion, "Boys, how would you like a
little sister for a birthday present?" Once all three of his
children had arrived safely and my mother was known to have
survived with no complications, all was well for him.

Because I knew my father less well than my mother, that
vanished, distant world now seems to me to be more his than
hers. While she stayed home to take care of us in our childhood, he left in the morning, returned for lunch, and came
back just after 5:00 p.m. from the Woodstock Electric Company, an event Howard and I eagerly awaited by standing together
on a chair Mother placed for us at the door, where we could
look through the glass and watch for him to turn the corner of
the house and come up the walkway. Sometimes he'd bring a
new box of crayons or a coloring book or a couple of little
metal cars or trucks he had picked up at the Economy Store on
his way home. In the evening we would all be together, How-

ard and I playing on the living room rug, Mother listening to the radio or record player with Poppa or darning or sewing. Once in a while he would get up and go to the hall to reach in his coat pocket and bring out a Bolster chocolate bar, a precursor of Butterfinger, and unwrap it for us and deliberately make the mistake of biting into the stiff black backing paper instead of the chocolate bar and then make a face and pretend to spit to make us laugh before he's split the bar in half and give us each our share. At bedtime Mother would read us a story, maybe *Stewy Slinker* or *How the Rhinoceros Lost Its Skin,* and then Poppa would appear to say goodnight to us, a ritual which would sometimes include his swinging each of us back and forth in his arms to "A rumpty-tump, a rumpty-tump, a rumpty-tump," and then with a final "a rumpty-tumpty TOLL-TAH!" he would toss us onto the bed so that we bounced. Then there was the roughness of his whiskers on our cheeks as he hugged us goodnight.

If as children ours was a somewhat sheltered life, I suppose that was partly the result of the accidental death of my father's five-year old brother and partly an expression of my mother's inclination to protect us. And we were somewhat sequestered by the place where we lived. The upper end of Pleasant Street and all of Elm Street and Benson Place were inhabited almost entirely by older couples and widows, so that Howard and I and eventually Jane were about the only children in the neighborhood. On summer evenings Poppa and Howard and I used to go down to the back lawn with our ball gloves for a game of toss and catch with a sponge rubber baseball. I remember once—we must have been in second or third grade at the

time—when a classmate of ours came over from his house on
Maple Street, a part of town teeming with children and very
near to Vail Field with its baseball diamond and football field
and its organized activities for children. My father surrendered
his place in the game to this boy and let him introduce the real
baseball he had brought with him. He threw hard, and though
our hands stung and we were pretty intimidated, Howard and I
did our best for a while so that word wouldn't get back to our
friends that we were a couple of sissies. My father, I remember,
watched us and encouraged us but did not see the moment as
any sort of initiation which ought to be followed by more of
the same, and we went back to the rubber ball in our games
with him. Neither did he encourage us to join the Boy Scouts,
and though he and my mother signed us up for Red Cross
swimming lessons at Barnard Lake, they immediately withdrew
us when we came home badly frightened by our first lesson in
which our instructor began by dunking the heads of all the
beginners in the lake. My father was furious, and assured us
that was not the way to teach young people to feel at home in
the water, and he trusted we would learn to swim in our own
good time. When we reached the age for kindergarten, my
parents did not enroll us. So, free from adult-supervised
activities, we spent our days as we wished in the small wood
across the road, along the banks of Kedron Brook, and down
on the land occupied by Frost's Mill along the banks of the
Ottauquechee River, and on the spacious lawns of the Fisk
estate that bordered our back yard on the north. We were free
to explore, to invent our own games, and we were allowed to

be bored and to discover reverie, which is the beginning of the inner life and the world of the imagination.

Only in recent years have I realized that I am as much indebted to my father as to my mother for the gift of my childhood years. It was to him that I owe much of my love of beauty and my sense of the sublime, for Woodstock was more his place than it was my mother's, and although he never said as much directly, I know he had a great and abiding love for the village. He quietly introduced us to places which he left uninterpreted, trusting us to intuit what they offered. On Sunday walks in our pre-school years, rather than choosing Vail Field or the elementary school playground, my parents would take us down Elm Street with its great houses and over the bridge and up Billings Hill, that elevation along Route 12 which offers a westward view of the front of the Billings mansion with Mt. Tom rising behind it, and an eastward view of the Billings Farm fields stretching to the Ottauquechee, flowing through its broad valley with Blake Hill in the distance. Was he in some way looking back into his own seldom-mentioned childhood during these excursions? Had he in his time been taken to these places by his mother and father? We didn't seem to be just wandering, but rather to be fulfilling some purpose. Unlike anyone I knew at the time, my father considered the grounds of the mansion to be public park land, so that we became early acquainted with formal gardens, statuary, marble fountains, manicured walkways bordered by clipped hedges, and we were captivated by open summerhouses and miniature ponds fed by man-made waterfalls. Had we been accosted by caretakers or members of the Billings or French families, and we never were, my father probably would have said we were simply making our way to the bottom of the Old Trail, which was one of the main routes up Mt. Tom in those days, and often that would have been the truth. But just as often we would spend the afternoons simply exploring the parkland and the fields and woods of the estate. In time, these adventures with our parents were followed by afternoons after school with an elementary school friend, Freddy Bradley, whose house on North Street occupied land contiguous with Mt. Tom and the grounds of the mansion. We were up there in all seasons, gathering moss and spring flowers for terrariums, playing Robin Hood or spying on Carl Bergstrom, the caretaker and our Sheriff of Nottingham, and his grounds crew. And in the winter, we carried our Northland skis up from Pleasant Street and put them on up there to cross the great lawns and climb to the sloped meadows and wide pathways above. Although the best place to go skiing in the village was the elevated part of the golf course, which offered a good, long, open ride from the fifth hole down to the fairway along the Kedron, it was not so much the greater distance from Pleasant Street that discouraged me from going there as it was a deeply felt distinction that the south side of town was somehow beyond the pale, unsanctified. It offered nothing to the imagination equal to the treks on skis, especially by myself, all around the Billings-French property, with the great house deserted in winter, its porches stripped of furniture, its gardens silent, its fountains filled with snow, the tall pine and spruce trees weighted down and offering secretive, bare spots as in other seasons, around their trunks in the gathering late afternoon light. Whereas my appetite for beauty perhaps originated in and was nourished by our early outings with my father, who must, in some way, have loved the places he introduced us to, whatever they meant to him remained a part of the essentially private person I felt him to be. Not so with me, but I never could find the words to express the inner world of thoughts and feelings these places inspired. I tried without much success to explain to my mother what happened to me as I stood on the Elm Street bridge and looked out over the snow-covered, ice-bound Ottauquechee at the sunset over Mt. Tom and recognized both in and somehow beyond that winter landscape, some promise of a world infinitely familiar and yet mysteriously other, or how I had suddenly seen cloud shapes in a patch of northern sky over the pine trees at the edge of our garden as a far off country, strangely familiar, that I needed to revisit. The experience was always the same: a sort of epiphany in which some thing or location was felt to reside in me, and at the same time, to open into a dimension beyond itself entirely. Mother would listen in a searchingly compassionate way and try to understand, knowing how important it was to me, and would sometimes ask my father to hear what I was trying to say. Though I had less faith in him, he would hear me and then shake his head as if it was beyond him. It certainly was not at all to my parents' discredit that they could not fathom what I was trying to make known to myself as well as to them, for, as Wordsworth knew so well, in these intimations of immortality when eternity breaks into time, "the child is father of the man." And un-doubtedly my efforts to reach out to my parents were too inarticulate to awaken in them memories of those "clouds of glory" in their own childhood and youth. Though I always felt that Mother came close to understanding me on the basis of her own treasured childhood on the farm in South Pomfret—and she certainly did not discourage me from seeking her out when I needed to talk about such things—perhaps any such experiences in my father's childhood lay buried on the other side of the harrowing events of the fall of 1923 that rushed him into a lonely life in his youth and early manhood.

However affectionate my father could be when we were children, intimacy as such was something I learned early not to expect from him or his brothers. He was not comfortable in hearing much about the inner life, and I have often wondered whether what Gaston Bachelard calls "the accumulation of silent things within us" ever prompted him to speak at length in any sort of confessional manner to my mother or whether his early stoicism served him all his life. It did not seem natural to me to be asking him to understand my exalted moments, and I would never consider reaching out to him from experiences of desolation, which were their antithesis. Homesickness was something I knew only too well, and it was an issue that, in my mind at least, divided my mother and father. Unlike my brother and sister, until I was in high school, I could go nowhere outside of Woodstock overnight without becoming absolutely miserable. The worst experience of homesickness, which taught me years later what my son Jonathan was experiencing in his boyhood times away from home, occurred when I was eleven years old and went to spend a week with a friend, Sandy Morse, at a lumber camp where his father was foreman in the Indian Lake region of New York state. Howard had been there with the Morses and reported a real adventure of canoeing, exploring the wilderness, and jeeping on logging roads, and it seemed like something I would enjoy. I got through the first night there, though not without feeling dreadfully far from home. But on the second day Sandy and I paddled a canoe in overcast weather and made little progress on wind-distressed, dark, and deep water surrounded by a huge and glowering wilderness with no beaches or dwellings in sight. And from then on things began to go badly for me in that outpost with its muddy roads and rough-hewn cabins and hoards of mosquitoes. On the second night as we settled into our bunks, the smell of Old Woodsman, the mosquito repellent we had put on that day and were still wearing, was frighteningly medicinal and threateningly claustrophobic and dark as though it were forcing me into some confined black space like the dark depths of that lake. It reminded me of my nightmare experience of having my tonsils out at Randolph Hospital when I was five years old: Howard and I were wheeled into the operating room, our hands were tied down, our faces were covered, and an ether-soaked cloth was taped over nose and mouth so that I could see nothing and could hear nothing except Howard's screams and my own as well. Then, plunged into darkness, I was assaulted by the terrifying images of ether dreams—suspended at a dizzying height near the ceiling of a cavernous and bottomless factory where great dark machines were grinding out geometric shapes that approached threateningly, then faded to be replaced by others. Something of that nightmare was being revived by Old Woodsman there in the cabin as it was just about time for lights out. Sandy's mother,

Lois, was a friend of my mother's and, of all the people I knew, most like her in warmth and understanding, and when she came in to say goodnight, I couldn't hold it in any longer and I a mixture of desolation and shame, began weeping. I knew that Bill Morse, Sandy's father, couldn't be expected to sympathize with me in the tough and masculine world of the lumber camp with its mostly Canadian loggers that he managed with determination and authority. I have thought often about that experience, the loneliness of it all, and it seems to me that my homesickness was exacerbated by my worry that there were feelings in me that would never be understood by people I cared about, such as my father and Bill Morse and so many other men who simply got on with things in their matter-of-fact lives. Lois, to her credit, did her best, rubbing my back and telling me it would be better tomorrow, though I knew it wouldn't. After one more such night, a phone call to my parents resulted in their decision to drive most of the distance in a car they borrowed from Uncle Jim, and rescue me. I knew that when they received the call they would be divided on what they should do. My father and, I'm sure, Bill Morse, would be in favor of making me stay put to weather my homesickness so as to conquer it once and for all—Howard had had no trouble, what was the matter with me? But my mother, who had also been afflicted with homesickness as a child, talked my father around. She was sympathetic when they picked me up at the spot where the Morses had agreed to meet them, though not as sympathetic as I might have wished. My father said little; he kept his feelings to himself. I am sure that, in light of his suffering in the fall of 1923, he must have thought that a few nights away from a home and family to which he could soon return ought to be possible for anyone to manage.

I am and am not my father. When in my time I was confronted with what to do about a homesick child, I did not hesitate for a second to help him; and my wife, who had experienced homesickness as a child, offered no resistance. Our like-mindedness led us to carry out if not actual rescue missions with Jonathan, at least such compromises as enabled him to better weather the distressing situations he was in. Interested in attending summer music camps, he twice managed to convince himself that he'd be able to stay away from home for a week's duration with no ill effects. One of the requirements of the choir camp in central New Jersey was that campers could not call home until the fourth day. When we answered our phone in Connecticut on that day and Maria spoke with him, his voice began to break, and in spite of his best efforts, he began to weep. Just as I had been at Indian Lake, he was both dreadfully homesick and very much ashamed about being so. Much more my mother than my father, I was all for going and bringing him home at once, but Maria wisely worked out a compromise with the directors of the camp whereby she would go and stay with her sister, who lived nearby, and take him back to her house at night so that he could complete the program as a day camper. When she arrived on the evening after his phone call, she realized how miserable he had been, for she found him in the same t-shirt and pair of shorts he had put on to leave home. Asked why he had not changed his clothes, he reluctantly explained that when he had opened his suitcase once for that purpose and had seen how carefully she had packed his things, it so greatly increased his misery that he zipped it up tight and put it out of sight, and it stayed that way. Something similar happened when four years later Jonathan again went away, this time about an hour and a half from home to Laurel Music Camp in Winsted, Connecticut for a week. During that time Maria was at a conference in Knoxville, Tennessee, and after a couple of days, Jonathan telephoned to say he was having a hard time of it but wanted to stick it out until the end and the final concert, for which all the campers had been rehearsing. So, only half-convinced by my father's inclination to let us face hardship as a way of learning fortitude and self-reliance, I set off every day to spend with my son the free hour the campers were given after lunch. From the moment he saw me sitting there in the car in the parking lot, I could sense his relief, just as I could sense his darkening spirits as the hour passed all too quickly. We simply sat there in the car, eating some of the peanut butter Nabs I had brought him, and talked, and I listened to his feelings as he explained them to me: he'd have been all right, he said, had it not been for the dreary shelter in which he slept, or tried to sleep. And suddenly, I was so completely back in the world of Indian Lake that while I was trying to lighten his mood I was reliving my two days and nights with the Morses in the dark cabin in the wilderness. Once when Jonathan was six years old, he told his mother, "Dad and I are the same. We have the same toes and the same little fingers. We can both use our left hands, and we have the same feelings." The best I could do during those fleeting noon hours at Laurel Music Camp was to let him know that his extreme sensitivity to place as indistinguishable from homesickness was something in my own life that he was helping me to understand in a way I had not been able to until then. I had no answers for him, and perhaps that was just as well. Solutions can preclude those experiences of opening up to each other and wondering out loud that are, at least for a time, respites from loneliness, assurances that "we are the same."

Although I cannot recall any such moments of affinity with my father, who was not at all comfortable in talking about his feelings, I did experience moments of intense sympathy for him. I had all but forgotten them until I overheard Maria talking about her youth with our children. She was remembering how self-conscious she felt in her bathing suit in her early teens, and how excluded when she could not swim well enough at the lake to reach the raft where her popular classmates were gathered. I happened to notice at that moment the expressions on the faces of Jonathan and Lizzie, and I realized that though Maria herself had pretty much put those experiences behind her, both of our children were suffering intensely for her and feeling helpless in the face of events from such a long time ago. And I remembered suddenly my mother's telling me, when I was in elementary school, about something that had happened recently to my father. He was walking home from work at the end of the day, carrying a bag of potatoes, and the bag split, spilling its contents onto the sidewalk. He had to make the best of it by gathering them all up and stuffing as many as he could into his jacket pockets and then trying to carry the rest rolled up in the remains of the bag. The slapstick potential of this moment, which, I confess, is evident to me now, was not so back then. Mother told it quite matter-of-factly, though not, of course, without sympathy, but, unknown to her, I was so overcome with sadness for him that I had trouble getting to sleep that night, imagining his embarrassment and helplessness there by himself with no one to assist him. Years afterwards I told my mother about it, and she was astonished at how I was affected by it, as I am sure my father would have been had I told him, which, of course, I would not have thought of doing. Then too I remembered one evening down on Pleasant Street when Howard and I were playing toss and catch on our way up from the back lawn to the house for supper, and Poppa, just having called us in, was standing on our walkway, watching us. A high school classmate of his, Fred Maynes, was just coming out of his sister Ada Maynes's apartment when one of us fumbled and dropped a throw, and Poppa said, good-humoredly, "Come on, hang onto it." Hearing him, Fred said, "You're one to talk; you weren't so hot yourself twenty years ago." I'm sure now that Poppa took it as a joke, as good-natured ribbing, but I instantly felt terribly sorry for him. I knew from what people had told me that he had been a very good high school second baseman, and I imagined that Fred's remark had wounded him and embarrassed him in front of his children, though I am now certain it really didn't. I was so upset about it I mentioned it to Mother, who, in some annoyance, told me Fred had been no athlete, and what's more that he was a fool who sometimes said thoughtless things, and she assured me that my father was not one to let anything like that bother him, and no feelings had been hurt.

In both of these instances, my sympathy for my father prompted me to go to my mother with my worries and my concerns. He was someone who didn't reveal much about himself, and someone, I felt, who would not be comfortable in hearing someone else doing that. What contemporary poet Chris Forhan says about his father in his memoir *My Father Before Me,* captures, quite remarkably, something of my relation to my father. Whatever could be said about his virtue, "In helping us to fathom and navigate our inner lives, he was not [expert]. In this way, he was a typical father of his generation. . . . But I suspect that his particular skill at silently, implicitly discouraging discussions of feelings was sharpened by his own childhood series of losses. . . ." I was someone who needed to talk about just that, my feelings. In fact, in this regard, throughout our childhood I think I was the more difficult twin for my father to understand. I was too loud, too extroverted; I noticed far too much and wanted to talk about the impression things made on me. If and when I found myself doing so with my father, even in the midst of saying, or just after having said, very little, I felt as though I was talking too much. At such times, he'd have preferred, it seemed to me, more restraint in my nature and my conversation. Around the Coffins, self-possession was the norm, and when my father and Howard and I were together, I certainly felt it was the order of the day. There we were, the three of us, on a bright and sunny day strolling through Boston Common before our first Red Sox doubleheader at Fenway Park, as though with a particular, serious purpose, not saying a great deal. It was Howard's and my first time ever in a big city, and my attention was everywhere, particularly—as it has been all my life—on human faces, and here, even in primarily white Boston, was a variety of color and shape I'd never experienced in monochromatic, waspy Woodstock. I stared at people, African Americans, Asians, people of Middle Eastern extraction, looking them in the eye, my fascination getting the best of my manners, and sometimes their gaze met mine. Had I just received an answering look of curiosity, or was it suspicion or hostility? Had that one man smiled because he thought perhaps I was funny looking? What if I were to become separated from my father and my brother among all of these strangers? Would any of them even have listened to my appeal for help? Who were they all, anyway, and where and how did they live? In these huge buildings, simply ignoring each other, as they seemed to be doing here on the Common and in the Public Gardens, where people just walked by others with no sign of recognition? Were they happy? I wanted to sit down on a bench with my mother or with a friend and talk about all this. It never occurred to me to consult Poppa, for whom the city was not a new place, though he had spent only one year there some thirty years before that. He was strolling right along, blending in with the rest of the pedestrians, minding his own business, looking, as it were, straight ahead. Overcome by a sense of wonder at the size and strangeness of everything and at the astonishing mix of people, I worked at keeping up the pace. For I had learned that it was no good asking questions or making any sort of searching observations, or, God forbid, trying to express my feelings about what I was seeing. For Poppa would reply in a dismissive manner, and Howard quite likely would have looked at me askance with raised eyebrow at effusions that were hardly standard Coffin behavior. Feeling myself the odd man out on these excursions, I finally gave up after my last trip to Boston with them when I was around age 14 or so and my interest in baseball had been replaced by girls and cars and basketball and rock and roll. Now the objects of my attention included pegged pants, upturned collars, duck-tailed haircuts, customized cars, pretty girls. Before we boarded the train home in South Station, we were each allowed to buy a magazine for the trip, and in contrast to the sports magazine Howard selected, I chose quietly, but to their mild derision, one about Elvis Presley with a photo of him performing at the Memphis State Fair on the cover. I could weather their disapproval because I knew that as soon as I was back in the company of my friends I'd have a great time showing it to them. I was then at the age to try out different identities, and there was, I now recognize, a restlessness of spirit in me that my father simply did not understand. It was as though I had glimpsed something early, back somewhere in childhood, something enduring, without knowing what it was, and I had become separated from it and was in search of what would put me on its track.

That search resulted in a number of obsessions, none of which proved to be satisfying or enduring. My fixation on bicycles gave way to a fixation on clothes, neither of which my father seemed to understand. Was it necessary always to be customizing my bike in different ways, trying out new handlebars at different positions, spending my money earned from mowing lawns after school on chrome fenders, paint, and accessories such as mud flaps and different handlebar grips,

trying to make my Western Flyer look like a Schwinn when a
bicycle was just something to get you more quickly from one
place to another? Howard made do with his 24-inch bike, the
only one he ever owned, and never changed it at all except to
raise the seat as his legs grew longer. Why couldn't I be satisfied with that? And what was the fuss about clothes? When
Howard and I were in elementary school, buying clothes was
simply a matter of going into Mitchell's Store with my father
and trying on some dungarees down in the basement, then
coming up to look at them in front of the big mirror and hear
what Poppa and the proprietor Elmer Emery had to say about
the fit. Then maybe we'd buy a t-shirt—our choice of color,
green or maroon or dark blue—and that would be it. And
when we needed shoes, we went to Shurtleff's and bought
Keds or Ball Band sneakers or any kind of leather oxfords they
had in our size. But as time passed, clothes became the focus
of my close attention. I noticed that the jeans worn by the
older boys, when rolled up, showed a lighter color than the
rolls in the dungarees we always wore, and that certain kinds of
jeans had distinctive kinds of stitching on the back pockets—
W for Wranglers, a wavy line for Lee Riders, and most importantly, the wing-shaped V for Levis—and learned that these
were "western style," and unfortunately they were not made in
sizes for anyone my age. It was no use remarking on these
observations and distinctions to Howard or Poppa, both of
whom would ask what difference it made, clothes are clothes,
and I'd feel foolish for noticing such things. Then it was not
long before I was gazing longingly at clothes in the Montgom-
ery Wards and Sears Roebuck catalogues and going out to the

newly-opened Angwin's Men's Shop on Elm Street to admire
the stock of ivy league button-down shirts and plaid belts and
the trousers with the buckle in the back. Always sympathetic,
Mother would drive me to Putnam's Store on Route 5 in
Windsor, which had a better shoe selection than Shurtleff's.
Susceptible to fads, I had a sort of imitation leather jacket
when those were in style, a green and white campus coat, and
in their time, white bucks, black loafers, snap-jacks, bombers,
blue suede shoes, graduating finally, when I was in college, to
burnt ivories and logger boots. Looking back on it all from so
many years' distance, I can share my father's view that so much
attention to fashion is foolish, but so too is so very much of
what happens in youth and adolescence, and it was simply in
my nature at that time to have taken it all so seriously, just as it
was in Howard's to have ignored it, and just as it was for my
mother to have understood and sympathized and my father not
to have done so. As silly, and I suppose as vain, as my interest
in these things may have been, it was rooted in my tendency to
take notice of—and though I little realized it at the time, to
remember—everything. Attention is, I have come to think, our
most important human attribute: the philosopher Malabranche
calls it "the natural prayer of the soul," suggesting therein that
its primary function in sponsoring the exchange between our
five senses and the details of the empirical world is revelatory.
And as Wendell Berry reminds us, attention is the basis of
imagination as the capacity "to see most clearly, familiarly, and
understandingly with the eyes, but also to see inwardly, with
'the mind's eye' not passively, but with a force of vision and
even with a visionary force." Growing up is, among other

things, a matter of selecting, somehow, from all that is stored
and illuminated in memory the enduring objects and the truths
of the heart that will enrich and direct the inner life over the
course of a lifetime. In that regard, when we are young, it is not
so much the things to which we attach importance, however
significant or trivial they may be, as it is the strength of the
attachment that counts and will see us through and eventually
save us.

If it was only my mother to whom I could try to articulate
these urgencies and intimate feelings, there was a kind of talk in
which my father could always be reached. The writer Brian
Morton says of a character in one of his novels that her father's
stories "turned [her] into a baseball fan. Baseball was a language she needed to know, because it was a language in which
her father revealed himself." For years when I was growing up
and afterwards, some of my most intimate—if such they could
be called—exchanges with my father had to do with sports at
all levels, midget and junior leagues, high school, college, and
professional. In high school he had been a good athlete
himself: second baseman, starting guard on the basketball
team, and he had excelled at track and field; he had set a school
record with a distance of over seventeen feet in the broad
jump. He was a good swimmer and a good skier. At tennis his
ambidexterity enabled him to hit forehand shots with both
hands. He was a good pool player who taught us the real
science of straight pool with its sophisticated combinations,
and his skill at bowling won him first place in a tournament in
Boston when he was at Wentworth. His best sport, however,
was golf, which he began playing as a boy. He had won a

caddies' tournament at the Woodstock Country Club when he was fifteen, and as a young man, he shot consistently in the low 70s, once winning a one-club-only tournament with that kind of score. I grew accustomed to hearing people of his time tell me that, had he dedicated himself to it, he could have gone on to a career as a professional golfer. Howard and Mother and I once went with him while he played eighteen holes by himself just to show us how it was done, and I once trailed him and a group of friends of his around in a match, but he pretty much stopped playing when we were young, and he sometimes spoke derisively of how seriously some people took the game of golf. Probably because of his success when he was young—unlike the late bloomer or the high school benchwarmer who needs to go on trying to prove himself in adult leagues when long past his prime—he had no trouble in retiring early from sports. And he never pushed Howard and me, but rather encouraged and helped us as he could when we showed a lively interest in a particular sport.

As both an athlete and a sports fan, he had an aesthete's understanding and appreciation for the beauty of the game or the match when played best, and while we were listening to baseball and basketball games on the radio with him, Howard and I would encourage him to tell us about the great major league players he had seen in Boston. His voice would grow thick as he recalled going early to Braves Field to watch first baseman George Sisler fielding grounders and taking throws during infield practice, which he said was like watching ballet. He had seen many of the legends of the 1920s, and though an avowed Red Sox fan all his life, he harbored an unspoken admiration for the Yankees as a result of having seen Gehrig and Ruth, and he could never forget the great arm of outfielder Bob Meusel. I suppose it was, in part, my desire to be thought of and spoken of in this way that made me want to become an athlete. I wished for some of the praise he bestowed on a fifth-grade classmate of mine when we were discussing the midget league tournament games, from which Howard's and my teams had been eliminated early. In bed that night, I lay awake for a long time, miserable with envy and jealousy, ashamed of having spent so much time on the bench, and before I finally fell asleep, I decided I was going to do all I could to become a basketball player. I set about doing just that, spending less time on other sports, practicing incessantly in all seasons anywhere I could find a hoop and a ball indoors or outdoors. I became a gym rat, attending by myself the high school team's afternoon practices to study all the moves of the varsity boys, and if I was lucky, to get in a few shots before the manager gathered up the balls while the players were showering. Poppa responded by taking us to Dartmouth College games, something no other father in Woodstock did with his children, so we could see basketball played at a different level entirely by the Dartmouth Ivy League championship teams of that time against opponents which included a number of All Americans. Through junior league and on into high school, I had improved my game steadily until I became a starting player and a scorer on the junior varsity team. I suppose my father's and my best moment occurred at the end of my sophomore year in the finals of a sophomore tournament in which we came up against Rutland High School on their home court. It was an opportunity to compete against a team in the 'L' division, representing the largest schools in the state, as opposed to the 'I' or intermediate division in which our teams regularly played. Early in the game, we fell behind, and sometime in the second half, our starting center and our point guard both fouled out, putting us down to substitutes who had played very little J.V. basketball. Rutland had kept the baseline closed with their 2-3 zone, and as right forward I couldn't get open for a shot anywhere along the right side of the court. Our coach had been unable to make adjustments and to find an offense that would work for us. Twelve points down with a little over three minutes to go, we were in a bad spot. Then reserve center Dave Harrington sank two foul shots to cut their lead to ten. As he stepped to the line, I happened to look up into the stands and noticed to my astonishment that my father, who never did anything that would attract attention to himself, was standing up and evidently trying to catch *my* attention. Swinging his arm in a semicircle, he was gesturing me to get out of the corner and cut to the top of the key. I began doing so, and I never missed: two quick jump shots, which brought the defense out and gave me the chance for a couple of layups, followed by two more jumpers—twelve straight points to give us a two-point victory. The jubilation at the end of the game was great, but what I remember best was the excitement after I returned home that night. My father was as ecstatic as I was and understandably proud of the part his coaching had played in our come-from-behind win, and I was beholden to him. And Howard, who had taken up sports writing in the town newspaper, gave me great coverage the next day.

However, as I came to learn, my father had little patience with anyone who took sports too seriously. From the moment I became a proficient scorer in basketball, I was almost more competitive with myself than with the opponent. Winning or losing for me was primarily a matter of succeeding or failing to live up to my own high expectations. A bad shooting night was a dreadful letdown and—since I couldn't leave the game behind me at the gym and brought my misery home—a source of contention with my father. If my mother's efforts to commiserate and encourage me were ineffectual, he would become exasperated and tell me to "stop bellyaching or quit playing." The latter was not an option: I had my whole identity wrapped up in becoming a great basketball player, and when I was not that—girls and rock and roll and friends notwithstanding—I was nobody. School bored me immeasurably. I had no interest in studying and no idea how to do it, received some low grades, and was gaining a bad disciplinary record. The new union high school, which opened in the fall of my sophomore year, looked like a prison to me, with its long, locker-lined corridor of classrooms resembling cells. Architecturally, its one-story sprawl was purely functional and aesthetically ugly inside and out, as was its setting two miles beyond the pale of the village of Woodstock on an undistinguished flat piece of converted field. I had loved the old high school building on South Street with its creaking stairways and high ceilings and had looked forward to my time in the upper classrooms with their cultured ambiance as a kind of rite of passage. Instead, for my sophomore and junior years, I moved up and down the long, fluorescent-lighted hallway from one cinder block enclosure to another until the last bell signaled the time for my escape. In retrospect, the odd thing was my parents' lack of serious concern over my report cards and my future. My father more or less left these matters up to my mother, who questioned me about low grades and actually sympathized with my complaints about boring and incompetent teachers. Having eschewed post-war middle class values and scoffed at the new obsession with acquisition and respectability and material well-being, they never pushed us to succeed or initiated conversations about what we might want to do after high school. It was up to me to continue trying on one persona after the other until, if I was lucky, I would find and recognize the one that corresponded somehow to the secret life of the soul that had long been waiting for its image, and is all that matters. Though I did not realize it at the time, something new had momentarily entered my ongoing sports dialogue with my father. In the summer before my last year of high school, I enrolled in a one-week session at Bob Cousy's basketball camp in New Hampshire in hopes of taking my game to another level. Dazzled there by the play of the college players who served as counselors and finding myself to be pretty average among campers from all over the eastern states and even the Midwest, I was as much a spectator as I was a participant during that week. Restless during the mandatory rest hour in the middle of the day—a presage of Jonathan's experience at music camp many years later—I was released to go down to center court where I might be able to make myself useful. When I got there, Holy Cross coach Lester "Bus" Sheary was working with Togo Palazzi— his former All American, who had been drafted by the Celtics and was then with the Syracuse Nationals—on his offensive game, and they asked me to rebound his shots. Completely star-struck, I was taken back five years to our living room on Pleasant Street, where Poppa and Howard and I huddled around the radio to listen to the finals of the NIT tournament from Madison Square Garden. The game put Holy Cross with Palazzi and stand-out sophomore Tommy Heinsohn up against a heavily favored Duquesne team with its three All-Americans, Dick Ricketts, Jim Tucker, and Sihugo Green. Miraculously, Holy Cross somehow pulled off the upset. Now, with the camp in its rest hour, there were just the three of us there on the court. Sheary, a basketball wizard, had an explanation for every missed shot, and I listened to him instruct Palazzi on footwork, release, follow-through, all the fundamentals. Then, after these sessions, Sheary had time for me, and we sat and talked basketball. He had coached Cousy at Holy Cross, and he told me that he had taken a particular interest in him from the moment in his freshman year when he showed up in his office and informed him that he wanted to be the greatest basketball player in the world. Sheary recalled telling him straight away that he'd first of all need to develop his left hand: "open doors with it, use it for the salt and pepper, eat with it, carry your books, answer the phone with it, etc." Under Sheary, Cousy realized his dream, and he never lost his reverence for his mentor. Cousy was the most ferocious competitor I have ever seen, a man who could not stand to lose or to put in only an average performance. I saw him kick a basketball all the way from center court nearly to the lake at the beginning of a time out after he had just missed a shot in a counselors' game, and the whole camp go silent. Though his anger at himself was just short of frightening, he would still listen to his old coach as if he were a boy, just learning the game. It was during my conversations with Sheary that I learned the strategies by which Holy Cross had overcome Duquesne: an elaborate, shifting variation of the box and one defense to contain Ricketts and Tucker and a dogged coverage of Sihugo Green by little Joey Liebler, who overplayed his right side and forced him to go to his left hand, which was his weakness. These mid-day sessions and conversations began to take precedence for me over my own less than satisfactory performance, primarily because I kept thinking about the interest and amazement my father would show when I told him about them. And when I got home, he didn't disappoint me, for his reaction was even greater than I expected it would be: "Well, is that so, you were right there with them, just you and them," and he'd shake his head in wonder: "Well, I'll be darned!"

I had not performed to my own high level of expectation at Camp Greylag, but I had come back with a story, and I had told it in such a way as to captivate my father. School began shortly after that, and I found myself in the English and European History classes of an extraordinary teacher, Harold Raynolds. He was sophisticated, well-traveled, articulate, highly educated, refined, passionate about his subjects; and he seemed to be interested in me, or rather to believe in some higher version of myself that he had spotted. He assigned free writing—a story, followed by a personal essay. Inspired and wanting very much to please him, I wrote a short story from the point of view of a survivor of the Blitz in London and an essay about my experiences with Togo Palazzi and Bus Sheary, both of which earned his high praise, and I gave a series of oral reports on members of the Nazi high command, which, I heard later, he raved about afterwards to some of his no doubt bewildered colleagues—former teachers of mine—in the faculty room. More importantly, through him I discovered literature, and education suddenly touched my inner life. It happened on a fall afternoon after school at the Woodstock Recreation Center when I was waiting with a friend to start a game on one of the pool tables there and remembered I had a reading assignment due in a few days' time. My friend happened to have his copy of the book with him, and I picked up the battered paperback and turned to the opening sentences: "A Saturday in November was approaching the time of twilight and the vast tract of unenclosed wild known as Egdon Heath embrowned itself moment by moment," and read on to "The distant rims of the world and of the firmament seemed to be a division in time no less than a division in matter," and the rest of that magnificent piece of landscape writing that opens Thomas Hardy's novel *The Return of the Native*. Here was someone who understood and shared all I had felt and tried at times to convey to my parents about those strange moments of illumination I had experienced from childhood on. Through years of homage to false gods, those epiphanies from the beginning had been signaling my life to me, directing me to a world of images and ideas as the true and enduring object of my attention, and I never looked back from that moment. My announcement to my parents that I wanted to go to the University of Vermont to study English and history stunned them, but once they understood my earnestness and saw in my grades evidence of my newfound purpose, they did everything they could to support me and make it possible for me to realize my aspirations. I have never ceased marveling at how much luck seems to have been on my side in the timing of it all. Harold Raynolds was in the Netherlands on a Fulbright fellowship in the year 1958-1959. Had that fellowship been for the next year, or had Howard and I been born two weeks earlier and been enrolled in school in 1947 rather than 1948, I would have missed having him as a teacher, and my life would have been different. And if acting high school principal Les MacDonald had not stepped down at the end of my junior year and been replaced by a new man, T. Chubb Condict, who decided to ignore the record and let us all begin with a clean slate, I don't know what college could have been persuaded, even by the best of Raynolds' efforts on my behalf, to accept me. In this awakening, I was as much of a surprise to myself as I was to my family, teachers, and friends. Years later, it was Uncle Jim, in an unusual moment of disclosure, who said it most succinctly. I had just received my M.A. in English from NYU and was home for a month in between two years of teaching in London, and he came up to Lincoln Street to see me. We spent some time catching each other up on the news, and then just as he was leaving and we were shaking hands, he said, "Well, I wouldn't have bet on you."

Of my parents, it was my mother who had the better understanding of what was driving me. She was a reader herself and had a wonderful appreciation of literature, and she went on to read the novels and short stories and poems that excited me.

In fact, when the date of Guy Fawkes Day came around, either she or I would sometimes write or telephone to say, "A Saturday in November was approaching the time of twilight...," in recollection of my awakening to literature. My father was pleased with my academic achievement, and he was always more proud of my college degrees than I was. I deeply regret to say that when it came time to have my graduation photo taken for my college yearbook, I considered it so unimportant that I neglected it altogether. Had I known how disappointed he would be when he opened the book and looked in vain for it, I would certainly have had it taken. He would sometimes show some curiosity about my interests in college, and he would listen as I tried to explain and would shake his head as though in bewilderment but also in approval and wonder. When he had heard a little of what I had to say, he smiled his approval and said something like, "You're doing well," and that would be it. And we'd both feel a little bit relieved. More often than not, our conversation at that point would drift back to our lingua franca, that is, to sports, where our sensibilities came together and we shared an aesthetic understanding. So much so, that it nearly got me in trouble on the day that Jonathan was born. When Maria was pregnant, it occurred to me that this would quite likely be the last of the Coffin grandchildren, and unless the child were a boy, the Coffin name would be discontinued in our line. When I mentioned that hope to my father, he seemed unconcerned, and I suspected that once again his first and only concern was for the health and safety of Maria and the baby, whatever gender it turned out to be. While Maria was in labor in Waterbury Hospital on 11 March 1979, I was seated outside the delivery room in the meager remains of what, as recently as five years earlier when my daughter was born, had been known as "pop's corner." It had then included a comfortable couch and an upholstered chair, vending machines for sodas and snacks and coffee, a supply of sports and news magazines, and a good-sized television set with an up-to-date *TV Guide*. But thanks to the capitulation of husbands to the new fashion of assisting wives in delivery, pop's corner had shrunk to a single chair and a TV set, and that was all. I was seated on the edge of that chair, watching the quarter-finals of the NCAA basketball tournament. Less than a minute after the end of the game, in which Ivy League University of Pennsylvania had pulled off the greatest upset in NCAA history by beating the nationally ranked, heavily favored Tarheels of North Carolina, a nurse appeared to tell me I had a son. I was already out of my seat at that time with excitement over the upset, and this additional news made me go nuts momentarily and start shouting and slapping the walls in elation. When I went in to see Maria and have my first look at Jonathan, she had just hung up the phone from announcing the glad news to her parents, and I wanted to call mine. They were as excited as I was, and Poppa admitted he was happy to know the Coffin name would be passed on to another generation. But, unfortunately, moments later when Dr. Kharma, who had delivered Jonathan, entered the room to check on Maria and congratulate me, our telephone conversation had turned to the subject of the game. And the good doctor, overhearing what I was saying, was annoyed enough to ask Maria if he could sit me down to speak with me about the significance of my son's birth. Poor Maria was required to assure him that I was appropriately relieved and excited by Jonathan's safe arrival and to explain to him as best she could, the marvelous convergence of events by which the final buzzer of a historic basketball game had been the signal for the Coffin name-bearer's emergence into the world. She reported that her efforts left him satisfied, placated, but somewhat confused, as would be the case for anyone who does not consider basketball a religion. Basketball was Jonathan's birthright, and in good time, I was perpetuating the father-son tradition that had begun with my father's taking Howard and me to Dartmouth games by taking Jonathan and Lizzie to Ivy League games at Yale's Payne Whitney Gym.

Outside of that sports bond with my father, he was an essentially private person whose demeanor commanded respect and seemed to inspire in others not so much attempts to draw him out as efforts to honor his reserve. He did not like telephones, though he never said so. When he did use one, which was rarely because my mother answered and managed all the calls, he held it in an unfamiliar manner, as though not knowing quite how to align it with both his ear and his mouth, and wanting very much hang it up or hand it to someone else. If the phone happened to ring when he was closest to it, wherever my mother or my brother or sister or I happened to be in the house, at least one of us would barrel down the stairs or race in from the porch or the back shed to answer it as though its ringing might disturb him or, heaven forbid, he might be compelled to pick up the receiver. It was a bit like the experience of taking him anywhere in a car. He was never critical of my driving, but when I was with him, I was very careful to stay within the speed limits and even to keep both hands at ten o'clock and two o'clock on the steering wheel as I had not done since the days of driver ed. In fact, my mother was the only one to criticize my driving, but only when he was in the car, as though she was worried that he was reluctant to mention something he might have been finding wrong with it.

Once, not long after Maria and I were married and were living in Woodstock for a year, she came to understand first hand something of this experience. As a church organist and choir director in Brandon, Vermont, Maria had to commute from Woodstock—a distance of fifty miles each way—twice a week for rehearsals and services and for other church events. Once, when she was called upon to play an afternoon funeral, my father surprised everyone by saying he'd quite like to go along with her and offered to drive her there. Some thirty-five years later when I told my sister about this, she said in astonishment, "He did?" I remember Maria appreciated the offer but was a bit intimidated about what they would find to say to each other all the way over to Brandon and back. Evidently, my father did not share her worry. I suppose they exchanged comments on the weather and the landscape they passed through. He may have talked about the improvements to Route 4 over Mendon Mountain since he had first known it as a dirt road dangerous to negotiate in the winter. Whatever they did or did not find to discuss, I'm sure that gaps in the conversation never bothered him, for he never talked just to fill a silence; in fact, silence was much more his element than talk for the sake of talk, and he disliked chatter. While Maria played the service that day, he visited someone he knew in Brandon, and they started home in the late afternoon. When he pulled out of the church parking lot onto Route 7, Maria, not being a Coffin, or rather not having been one long enough, or both, said, "Oh, no, I always go home over Brandon Gap." He was, she remembered, a little surprised, but he readily agreed, and that is the way they crossed the Green Mountains that day and returned home. She enjoyed the trip. There was a particular elm tree she loved in a pasture on some farmland, and she remembers his approval of her interest in it, evidence, perhaps, that though she was a city girl to him, she could understand and appreciate the beauty of the countryside. It was, I think, the only time the two of them were ever alone together for that length of time, and it was only after Maria had come to know him better—or not to know him better—that she couldn't believe she'd had the audacity to encourage him to do something outside of his customary ways, though he no doubt enjoyed the different scenery on that return trip to Woodstock. At least we chose to see it that way, and he never registered a complaint about the change of route. To my knowledge he never tried in any way to convey to anyone that he preferred to do things his way or to suggest that his quiet life was not to be altered or disturbed, but whether he knew it or not, that was the impression he gave. And not just to his family; I remember meeting and coming to know a young woman, Linda Hauge, who had moved to Woodstock and taken a temporary job as a waitress in a restaurant in the middle of Woodstock. When I was introduced to her and she heard the name Coffin, she greatly surprised me by asking whether my father sometimes had morning coffee at the Corner Dairy Bar. When I answered that he did, she winced a little out of embarrassment and said she was afraid that she had recently made his toast a little too dark for his liking. I knew that he never would have complained, but she somehow had quickly inferred that she was supposed to honor the way he liked to have things done. My sister told me recently that all her school friends were afraid of him and walked and talked softly in his presence, though he was always pleasant to them and actually enjoyed their being around the house.

Perhaps it was my father's quietness, his composure, that gave such a strong impression that he was not to be interfered with in any way. The Coffins kept their distance, and that tacit arrangement was something that Maria at first found difficult to understand. Coming as she did from a large Dutch family who settled in New Jersey in the early years of the 20th century, she was accustomed to frequent family get-togethers on both her father's and mother's side, and she wondered at a family who lived close together yet seldom saw each other except by chance or unexpected drop-in visits, and never by invitation. So, when we were living in Woodstock in 1971-72, it was natural for her to consider inviting my parents and Ralph and Uncle Jim over to our apartment on Slayton Terrace for supper. Since she had been around my father enough to know that even the smallest attempt to educate his palate was to be avoided, and she assumed his brothers too would prefer to be served what they were accustomed to eating, she sought my mother's advice about the menu. Now, while Maria was perfectly relaxed and looking forward to the event, Mother was feeling pretty nervous about the whole undertaking. However, she was willing to help in any way she could, and after considerable discussion, they settled on ham and green beans and scalloped potatoes and homemade rolls and homemade apple pie for desert. Maria recalls that at first my uncles were somewhat shy, but after a drink—we had bought scotch and beer for the occasion—in the living room before supper, they relaxed and became talkative. They also ate very well, greatly enjoying the meal, and they stayed on for quite a while afterwards for more conversation. At one point, early in the evening, I gave them all a tour of the apartment, which was oddly arranged because the house had been divided and subdivided so many times that the rooms of a single apartment could be widely separated. On the way to our bedroom, which was quite a ways off from the rest of our rooms and by itself in the main part of the house, we crossed an old, unlit and unheated front hallway with a wide, curving, banistered staircase that rose into a dark, unused landing on the second floor. Uncle Jim and Poppa stopped and gazed up the stairway and remembered sliding down the banister with their childhood friend Roger Slayton, who had lived there in the first two decades of the century. At the end of the evening, when it was growing late, Ralph and Uncle Jim expressed their gratitude and put on their winter coats to leave. We switched on the porch light and stood outside to see them out into the cold, and went back inside where Mother and Poppa were helping to clean up the dishes. And then they too left, and we watched their taillights disappear and looked off Slayton Terrace down into the snow at the lights in the houses on Ford Street and Pleasant Street. That fully furnished apartment, which we occupied for only five months, was perhaps the homiest place I have ever lived in. To recall now the lamp-lit living room with its paintings and prints and wall hangings and comfortable stuffed chairs and the small den crowded with books, which doubled as a guest bedroom, is to step back into that place just as it was on that night of the only Coffin family get-together of that sort that we ever had. It took someone from outside the family, Maria, to make it happen—the nervous excitement of Mother and me, the arrival of my uncles, the perfect meal, the conversation, the sense of accomplishment when it was over. And then, strangely, there was also that sense of relief, as though something could possibly have gone wrong among those three quiet, appreciative, well-mannered men, who would never have uttered a word of complaint or objection about anything; as though we might somehow have, if not actually offended, at least intruded upon some part of them that could never quite come to be known, going back to that unused hallway with its long dark staircase, serving no purpose then except to reach up into their lost childhoods, which they might momentarily recall but never speak about at length.

Because my father was so private, the moments when he came out of himself were memorable. Drink brought out the best in him by making him more gregarious, more talkative, and it certainly brought out his sense of humor. Except for the annual drink of whiskey with Haze at Christmas time, he limited himself to beer and drank only a few cans of Budweiser at home on a Saturday night. When Howard and I came of age, we greatly enjoyed imbibing with him. Our first such times were when we were home from college and would host big parties at Lincoln Street for our friends. I remember moments when he was suddenly overcome by laughter: a friend of mine Roger Glazebrook showed up at one of these events in a handsome tweed glen plaid sports jacket, white shirt, and bow tie, and baggy denim coveralls. Chuckling at the mismatch, my father asked him what he was wearing for shoes, and Roger adjusted the straps of his coveralls so as to raise the legs and reveal patent leather dancing pumps, the sight of which nearly convulsed him. At another such party, a large, warm, expansive friend of mine, Henry Summers, was standing a little unsteadily next to my father and gazing fixedly at the dining room table, evidently trying to focus his vision; suddenly, he sidled across that customary physical space between my father and people in general, draped a big arm around his shoulder—something I had never done and was never to do—leaned toward him in an affectionate and conspiratorial manner, and said, apropos of nothing, "Wally, goddamned aluminum siding really sucks." There was my father, caught in a sort of embrace, erupting in laughter. The intimacy and the spontaneity of that moment are unforgettable. Both he and my mother were so well loved and respected by our friends that they began to be invited out to parties even when Howard and I could not be in attendance. At one of them, held by a friend of ours in Prosper on a weekend when his parents were away, they had been heartily welcomed by the host and the crowd of college students and Poppa was working on his second beer when, as he told it, a chainsaw was heard starting up outside. Two young men had decided, evidently on a moment's inspiration, that they'd like to cut down a utility pole in a field near the house. In some doubt that anyone would do such a thing, a number of partygoers including my parents stepped outside and saw that the work was actually in progress. Being at that time an employee of The Vermont Public Service Corporation, my father, though greatly amused by this stunt, decided it would not be a good thing to be on hand if and when the police should arrive, so he stayed just long enough to finish his beer and see the pole come crashing down amidst a tangle of wires, before he and my mother left the scene. At work on the following Monday, when he was told about the severed pole, he feigned astonished disapproval, and over the years he never could recall the event without shaking his head and chuckling. In the same spirit is something that happened when I was touring the old Wood-stock Inn with him shortly before it was razed. Having made our way slowly through the great lobby and along the first floor with other people who were paying their last respects, and having toured the guestrooms above, and the tower, we went to the basement to have a last look at the bar, known then as The Pine Room. Just as we were leaving there, my father nudged me and directed my attention to something leaning up against a wall in a dark corner—one of the two "Pine Room" signs that used to direct clientele from the parking lot and from outside the front of the inn to the bar itself. I spotted it, and he looked at me out of the corner of his eye and raised an eye-brow. And, seeing what I was meant to do, I loosened my belt and slid the sign down the back of my pants, hiding the top part under my shirt and coat, and we exited the building and went home. It was our only father-and-son heist, and we saw it as salvaging rather than stealing, and gave the sign a prominent place in the house on Lincoln Street. We were both pleased with the caper which gave us a keepsake from that grand old building which, had it not been for the real crime of Laurance Rockefeller—Ada Louise Huxtable in the *New York Times* rightly called it "an act of vandalism"—would still be in its rightful place on The Green in Woodstock today.

Having foresworn tears early in life after the death of his little brother and his mother, my father nevertheless shed many in response to the fullness of his life. Humor brought them on, and, more fully and consistently, so did music, which, even more than sports, was the great compelling interest of his life. I suspect it was an inheritance from his mother, who loved music and played the organ, and music may very well have brought her back to him in some way whenever he heard it. Though undemonstrative as he was—he never, as far as I know, sang a single note—he was a silent, or at most, a barely audible whistler. Like his brother Haze, he was an ardent Dixieland jazz enthusiast, but his passion was for opera. It began when he was a boy and used to listen to Caruso on the radio and on what records his parents had and could play on their old wind-up Victrola. Poppa had few experiences of live opera in his life, and I don't think he cared whether he listened to it in full performance or in concert as long as he was hearing the music of the great composers, Verdi, Puccini, Donizetti in particular, as I remember him doing when he was tuned in to "The Voice of Firestone" on radio and later on television. He would sit forward in his easy chair, listening in rapt attention, to Richard Tucker and Robert Merrill, Renata Tebaldi, Anna Moffo, Leontyne Price, Jerome Hynes and others. And he would repeatedly get up—in those days before remote controls—to inch up the volume a little more, tears leaking from the corners of his eyes, his throat so constricted he could hardly speak. It is one of my greatest regrets that I was not with him and the rest of the family in 1978 when they went to Spaulding Auditorium at Dartmouth College to hear a full recital by the then not so well known Luciano Pavarotti, and Poppa knew right from the first aria that he was in the presence of the greatest tenor since Caruso.

Music got inside my father and almost entirely possessed him. Like most true music lovers he did not listen to it every day, and he did not like background music. He also had a very good ear. In the summer of 1968, when Maria was enrolled in the New England Conservatory summer school at Castle Hill, the Crane estate on the coast of Ipswich, Massachusetts, she and I arranged it so that my parents could attend a performance of Mozart's *Cosí Fan Tutte*. It was to be performed by the students in a grotto in one of the estate's great formal gardens. The opera under the stars on that mild, clear summer evening was magnificent, and particularly impressive was the quality of the voices in the lead roles—Rafael LeBron, baritone, as Guglielmo; Jeanne Panther, soprano, as Fiordiligi; and Frank Hoffmeister, tenor, as Ferrando. But as memorable, if not more so, was something that occurred in the afternoon, hours before the opera itself, when we were giving my parents a tour of the estate. We were walking along the lawn at the side of the mansion when, through an open window, came the sound of a soprano warming up and singing some phrases. We caught a glimpse of her, but so as not to distract her, we moved in closer to the building and out of sight. My father stood there transfixed, as though miles away, completely lost in the sound, and for some moments afterwards he could not speak. Her name was Holly Outwin, and she was young at the time and did not have a role in *Così*, but my father said later that, much as he had enjoyed the opera, the highlight of his time in Ipswich was those moments on the lawn, and he always mentioned it when we recalled our experience at Castle Hill.

One night a number of years later, when I was visiting my parents after Christmas, I remembered to deliver a recent message from Maria to my father: "Tell Wally that, as it turned out, Holly Outwin, the girl whose voice he heard through the window of the Crane mansion, was the real rising star of all the talented singers at the Conservatory that summer." On hearing this, Poppa was simply overwhelmed; again, as when he was listening out there on the lawn, he was speechless; his eyes filled with tears, and, a little choked up, he said, "Is that right? Well, I'll be darned, I said so, I heard something I didn't hear in the others that night." And then he did something unusual for a person who did not like cold weather and always kept inside on winter nights, something he was never to do again. He stood up from his chair, looked at me, and to my mother's and my astonishment, said, "Let's go down to the Pine Room," and we did just that. And in the hour or so we spent there, we raised our glasses to Holly Outwin.

In as much as I credit my mother more than my father with an understanding of the life I discovered and went on to lead, I have come to think I owe him more than I realized during his lifetime. Though he was not a reader and did not value literature as my mother and I did, music was for him much more than simply entertainment. It was a passion, and it was inherited by all three of us, his children. Its transcendent power over him was experienced as a mystery. If he never spoke of it as such, it was because he had no words, and knew that there was no language for it. What music meant for him gave me a first glimpse of what all the arts would become for me— expressions of a reality much greater than that of the common, ordinary, workaday world, which made few claims on any of us in our family. He and my mother were two of the least materialistic people I have ever known. They attended to each other and to their children and grandchildren and to events in the natural world around them. My father lived for the long days of summer and was never happy at the end of foliage season with the prospect of early darkness and freezing temperatures, and he never liked the sight of falling snow. Each winter as it piled up and their world shrank until Ralph could plow the driveway and they could complete what shoveling was necessary after that, my father busied himself with small projects. He fought an annual winter campaign against the gray squirrels to keep them from stealing the seed he supplied his beloved chickadees and finches, but approved of the incursions of deer driven by hunger out of the woods to visit the feeder on the lawn. He and my mother kept a list of the birds they spotted, and he would often tell me in our weekly phone conversations about the visitations of a pair of cardinals. He loved to watch the smallest of the birds busily braving the cold and, with his assistance, getting on with their lives. Once they rescued an evening grosbeak from the jaws of a neighbor's cat and were relieved when, apparently not seriously harmed, it was able to fly away. Later that day, around dusk, it came back to a bush in the yard where they had never seen it before, and sang to them.

Summer was my father's time of year. He enjoyed mowing the lawn and reclaiming patches of grass that had been damaged by Ralph's snow plow, and bringing back parts of Bertha's extensive flower gardens. But his greatest interest was his raspberry patch, which he had created on the eastern border of our property beside our big lawn. Although it was not a large patch and it had been planted in places around some rocks that were too large to move, he took great care of all of his plants, and they were extraordinarily productive. He would go through them all, inspecting both sides of every leaf of every plant in search of Japanese beetles, which he would remove with a device he had created for that purpose by attaching two flat sticks to form something like giant tweezers. With it he could grasp the beetles and remove them without in any way damaging the leaves. He also kept a vigilant watch along the stems of his plants for cane borers, the berry patch's other chief enemy. The result of his careful husbandry was a bountiful annual crop of large and delicious red raspberries. Though his patch measured only some twenty-five yards in length by five yards in width, its yield was almost more than he and my mother could harvest. It was the job of only the two of them—though I offered several times to lend a hand at the height of the season—for they had a method, and my father was worried about the bushes being damaged by anyone unfamiliar with the lay of the land. Given these concerns, he was always surprisingly tolerant of the neighborhood children who sometimes poached from the edge of the road. If he caught them in the act, he shooed them away, but he always took them and their parents a gift of berries at the end of the growing season. In their best years they would harvest some 300 to 350 pints of berries. Of course, they ate some, and Mother made pies, and they gave some away to friends and relatives, but most of them were sold to faithful customers. From the patch, where they picked into shallow containers to prevent the weight of the top berries from crushing the ones beneath, they would take them up to a table and chairs on the porch to "pick them over." In this operation they touched every berry, and selected only the best ones for sale, placing each one in the basket in such a way the there were no spaces between them. And, unlike other sellers, they also heaped each basket well above the rim.

Though they sold most of what they picked and kept careful track of their yield and their profits, they were not really in the berry business for the money. I don't recall their ever selling to any store or farmers' markets; they simply didn't have to. The news of their berries spread so that they were never lacking in people who wanted them. Their main customers were Laurance and Mary Rockefeller, who bought their berries and no one else's in great quantities and insisted in paying a good fifty cents more than the asking price for each pint they were supplied. I think my parents could have sold almost exclusively to them if they had chosen to, but did not see why they should be given that privilege. We were told by their caretaker who came to pick up the berries that the Rockefellers kept them in a large silver bowl in the middle of the great dining room table in the mansion, where they were considered a delicacy on social occasions.

I don't think my father was ever called upon to explain why he put so much time and effort into his small berry patch every year in an enterprise that was nothing if not labor intensive. But had he been asked to do so, he might very well have said he was in it for the enjoyment and let it go at that. He most likely would have understood Frost's cryptic line, "The fact is the sweetest dream that labor knows," as a characterization of his complete absorption every year in his largely solitary enterprise. The growth of his raspberries and their coming to fruition after the bushes had endured sub-zero temperatures and been buried under snow every winter were for him, I am sure, like the cheerful activities of the chickadees on his feeders on the coldest days, the shy appearance of deer on his lawn, the annual return of one painted trillium in an otherwise derelict flower garden by the front porch, and the sudden spectacle of the maples setting the hillsides aflame with color each October—miracles he was devoted to honoring, and, in the case of his berry patch, serving in his own humble way.

I suppose it is singularly appropriate that one of my most enduring images of my father is of him overwhelmed, as it were, in a posture of surrender and gratitude among his berry bushes. Oddly, it comes not from direct experience but from something my mother told me. When Maria discovered that she was pregnant with our first child in 1974, the expected delivery date was September 10, Uncle Chick's birthday, which would have added another to our family's duplicated birthdays (my mother's older brother, Alan, was born on January 10, the same day as Howard and Jane and me; Haze and Bertha were both born on Christmas day). But evidently Lizzie had her own agenda about timely arrivals and decided to make her entry into the world several weeks early, on August 1st, my father's birthday. When I telephoned my parents from Connecticut early that afternoon with the news (they did not even know Maria had gone into labor on July 31), my mother answered the phone, and I said simply, "Ask Poppa how he would like a new granddaughter on his birthday." Speechless for a moment, she managed to collect herself and said, "Ohh, ohh I will; he's down in the berries." And I heard her call to him as best she could out across the lawn from the kitchen steps, her voice breaking, "Wally, Bruce wants to know how you'd like a new granddaughter for your birthday." There was a short silence, and then she was back on the phone again to say, "He's disappeared. He was standing up, picking, and suddenly I can't see him; I'd better go. I'll call you back." As reported a short time afterwards, she found him sitting on one of the large stones in the middle of his raspberry patch, completely overcome. Later that day, when he tried to tell a family friend who stopped at the house to buy some berries what had happened, it was simply too much for him, and he had to rely on Mother to deliver the news. Simone Weil says that "Grace fills empty spaces, but it can only enter where there is a void to receive it." I think that for my father the void created by what had been taken from him early in his life—which left him so bereft as to fear my mother's risking pregnancy at all—was such that the safe arrival of every child and grandchild left him feeling deeply grateful if not actually beholden.

It was characteristic of my parents that, while my mother liked nothing better than to go berry-picking up in the hills of Pomfret, where she was born and spent her youth, my father cultivated his own berries so that he did not have to travel out into the country and search for them. He enjoyed evening drives through the countryside on familiar roads, but he wasn't afflicted with wanderlust and a desire to explore new territory. And old habits died hard with him. Though the trip north on Route 5 along the Connecticut River to Fairlee, where he and my mother liked to stop at the Fairlee Diner, was about as long as the trip to Rutland, it was only in preparation for the latter that he would go out to A&B Motors to have his tires checked before starting out because that journey meant crossing the Green Mountains, a major geographical divide in his early days. And there were a number of years when their activities away from home were limited by their responsibility to Lura Metcalf, Bertha's younger sister, who came to live with them in her old age. Years before that time, Mother had given her an assurance that when she was too old to take care of herself, there would be a place for her there at 43 Lincoln Street in what had been the Metcalf house. When that time came, in 1965, she was true to her word from then until Lura died in 1975. Though it was difficult for my parents to be so bound to the house in these years, I'm sure my mother, who was the more adventurous spirit, felt the constraints more than my father, who was not one to travel. Between the time of Lura's death and the beginning of my father's final illness in 1979, Mother, I know, would have liked to visit us more often in Connecticut, but only if she had been assured that it was to my father's liking. Actually, once he had made up his mind to take the trip, he never complained about the distance or the traffic, but simply got on with it and evidently appreciated the change of scene. As it was, I think they made only two such journeys to see us in that time, and for some reason I can remember vividly only one of those visits. They came to spend Christmas with us in 1975, when Lizzie was not quite a year and a half old. So that they would be warm enough during their brief stay in the drafty old house on the campus of Westover School, where I was working at the time, we laid in a good supply of wood for the three fireplaces. Though as children we did not know it, my father was strangely ambivalent about Christmas, as we came to learn from things Mother told us when we were older. For one thing, during his years at the Woodstock Electric Company, by the time Christmas Eve had arrived, he was tired of working the required extra hours in the store, which stayed open nights for the two weeks preceding the holiday, and tired of the whole frantic business of retail in that season. And though he was susceptible to the beauty of Woodstock buried in snow and lit up by Christmas lights in the shops and houses, and could understand and perhaps even share in some of the excitement of his children, my mother thought there was a way in which the holiday saddened him by returning him to the distant world of his childhood and youth when his mother was alive and all the family, including his little brother Howard, were together. I suppose his Christmas with us in Connecticut was the only one he ever spent outside of Woodstock. At the time, we all had great hopes that he would enjoy it. As it turned out, we needn't have worried.

On Christmas Eve, as the sun was going down and the light was thickening over the playing fields beyond our back lawn and in the woods in front of the house, I needed to go to Middlebury Store for some last minute purchases, and my father—never one to go out into the cold if he could avoid it—surprised me by asking if he could join me. He had, I remembered, heard a great deal about that extraordinary little neighborhood business, which, even then was a vestige of commerce as conducted in an earlier time: charge accounts, best wishes and free candy on children's birthdays, even home deliveries to customers. In the store, as soon as I introduced my father to the proprietor, Tom Thomas, and the butcher, Howard Heaton, they promptly squired him off to the makeshift bar set up in the store's back room every year on the day before Christmas. I hurried my shopping so as not to leave him long in the company of people he had just met, but by the time I joined them, Poppa was sipping his annual Christmas glass of whiskey, and the three of them were talking like old friends. I think he had entered a kind of time warp in that small neighborhood grocery store and returned to the Woodstock of his earlier days. And the drink of whiskey may have taken him back to the Christmas Eves when he and Carroll ("Ben") Bennett, district manager of the Woodstock Electric Company, would close the store and go back to Ben's office for a couple of "nips" before going home. At any rate, by the time we had added two six packs of Schlitz to our purchases, wished the staff of Middlebury Store a merry Christmas, and headed home, he was in the best of spirits. In fact, so ready was he to carry on our celebration of Christmas Eve that after dinner he and I went to work on the Schlitz supply as we wrapped the last of the presents. In Maria's recollection, when she returned from playing the service that night at First Congregational Church in Cheshire, she was surprised to see all the lights in the house blazing and to discover, on entering, a bright-eyed Lizzie still up long past her bedtime and happily snuggling with my mother on the couch in front of the fire, admiring the lights on the Christmas tree. And there was Poppa, chuckling to himself and weaving toward the kitchen with his winter cap pulled down sideways over his head, the earflaps down, to make my mother laugh. And I too was well away. His happiness was infectious to us all, but particularly to my mother, who, in her way, always wanted things to be just right for him and was relieved to see him feeling very much at home in a place so far from Woodstock.

My father had been a cigarette smoker all his life. However, when Uncle Jim was diagnosed with emphysema, the two of them decided to stop smoking and did, though as my father was to learn in 1979, not soon enough. Unlike his brother, he decided to cooperate with his doctors, to follow their advice and have regular checkups, and to make use of oxygen to assist his breathing when necessary. Eventually, as physical exertion became more difficult for him, he gave up his short walks on Lincoln Street, and he and my mother took shorter outings in the car, with her doing the driving. The last time he actually drove their car was, I think, on a bright, clear October day in one of the last years of his life, when he surprised Mother by saying he was going to go out for a while. He evidently needed to experience by himself, perhaps for the last time, the old hills once again dressed in their crimson and gold. It was the height of the foliage season, and he was gone long enough for Mother to begin worrying about him and to be much relieved when she heard the car pull up into the driveway. He entered the house simply shaking his head, astonished once again at what he had seen, and began trying to tell her about it. Then he fell silent.

As the emphysema progressed, my father and mother's world grew smaller. Eventually, the long staircase to the second floor was too much for him, and with some assistance they moved their beds downstairs and lived primarily on the first floor. In the four years in which he suffered, Poppa never actually gasped for breath or appeared to be short-winded, but he was most comfortable not sitting in his chair as he always had done, but, instead, standing behind it and leaning forward with his elbows resting and supporting his upper body on the back of the chair. As he lost weight and his face became more drawn, he elected to take oxygen more often during the day as well as throughout the night. On our visits to Woodstock during this time, we stayed with friends or at Ralph's camp and made frequent stops at Lincoln Street, staying there only a short time because noise and activity in the house tended to tire my father out and to take his concentration away from the labor of breathing. Having been in Dartmouth Hitchcock Hospital once for observation and treatment, he finally decided that he would be more comfortable there than at home, and he and my mother moved there for his last days, arranging it so that she could have a bed next to his in his room and be with him at all times. And Jane sometimes stayed there as well to allow Mother to get some much-needed rest. Right from the beginning of his illness, my father made it clear that when the time came, no extraordinary measures were to be taken to prolong his life. One morning just a day or so before his death, he confronted the doctors making their rounds: "I should have died last night," he said, and he told them he suspected they had in some way gone against the agreement. In fact, he was right; someone on night duty in the early morning hours had introduced steroids into his intravenous fluids, and he let them know in no uncertain terms that that sort of thing was not to be done again. It was shortly after these events that I saw my father for the last time. On the afternoon of January 4, 1983, Howard and I arrived at he hospital to find him propped up in bed and my mother with him. We talked for a while about Lizzie and Jonathan and Howard's daughter Anya, assuring him they were well, and we spoke also of what was going on in sports and about the weather, just the sorts of thing we had always talked about on the phone. After a while, Mother asked him if he would like to rest, and he said he thought he would. So we said goodbye to him and told him we'd be back that night or the next morning. He reached out from his bed for a handshake, which was usually his way of saying goodbye when any of us were leaving the house after a visit. We shook hands. His grip was as powerful as it always had been, and we left for Howard's apartment in West Lebanon, only four miles from the hospital. When we arrived there and walked through the door, the telephone was ringing. Howard answered it and after a moment said, "O.K., then" and, still on the phone, extended his hand to me. I grasped it and hung on while he continued speaking into the receiver. He said, "We'll be right along," and then he put down the phone and said simply, "That was Mother; he's gone." So we returned immediately to the hospital and found her there in the room with his body. As she was calmly gathering up his things and waiting for the orderlies to wheel him away, a candy striper came in, cheerfully pushing a cart with trays of food on it. "O.K., Mr. Coffin, it's time for a little afternoon snack now," she chirped. Howard said, "Uhhh . . . I don't think Mr. Coffin will be needing anything to eat." She looked at him quizzically and then looked at my father, and her eyes widened, and she raised her hand to her mouth and said "OHHH!" and wasted no time in spinning around and wheeling her little cart out into the corridor and away. It was, I realized, a moment Poppa would greatly have enjoyed and the first of many times throughout the years since his death when something that would have amused him has made me feel strongly his presence in his absence. Then it was time to leave. The three of us exited the room and began what was for me the very strange experience of walking down the long corridor to the elevator and then out along the first floor hallway to the main lobby on our way to the front entrance. We went along in succession with Mother leading the way, followed by Howard, with me behind them. She walked resolutely, as did Howard and I, but I couldn't believe, somehow, that we were able to advance, to go away from that room, and by putting one foot in front of the other—I was supremely conscious of the actual physical process of walking—begin moving forward into the rest of our lives.

In the days between his death and his funeral, Maria and I and the children stayed at Lincoln Street with my mother. As I was running a low grade fever and feeling listless, Howard and Ralph took care of the funeral arrangements, making sure to honor my father's last wishes, which specified the cheapest possible obsequies. The service took place on the afternoon of January 7 at the North Pomfret Church with Pastor Doris Rikert, an earthy and compassionate woman, officiating. Maria played on the organ the pieces we had selected, which included "Green Sleeves," the Shaker hymn "Simple Gifts," and Bach's "Sleepers Awake." It was well attended by members of my mother's family and by my parents' friends from the old days, and we chose my cousins Philip and John Biathrow and Jim Jillson and my old friends Dave Doubleday and Sandy Morse and the son of our Lincoln Street neighbors, Dave DeTurk, as bearers. It was a service which we felt would have pleased my father. Had I been able to select a requiem to be performed at that time (the very idea of anyone's even thinking of making that kind of fuss would have seemed absurd to him), it would have been that of Gabriel Fauré, which, with its lovely "Pie Jesu," has always seemed strangely suited to the quiet and essentially private nature of my father's character.

My parents were not, in any conventional sense of the word, religious people. That is, they did not belong to a church or have much regard for public, communal worship. In fact, my mother was baptized in the Christian Church in Woodstock when she was an adult only so that Howard and I and Jane could be baptized, as the church had a ruling that only the children of baptized parents could receive that sacrament. Her family, the Jillsons, resembled most closely Unitarians. In her childhood and youth up on the farm in South Pomfret, they had said prayers, read the Bible, and sung hymns in the evening before bedtime, but only rarely made the trip into the village for worship services. Years later, after my mother's sister Julia became Roman Catholic because her son had converted, she told Mother that though it fulfilled some spiritual requirements of her nature, as a religious experience, Catholicism could not begin to compare to what they had had on the farm. I know much less about this aspect of my father's upbringing. I suppose he attended Sunday School at the Methodist Church or the Christian Church in Woodstock, and he and Mother had the three of us children baptized, though that was, as I learned later, primarily to please Grammy Coffin. My father never went to church except to see us as children participate in a Christmas pageant or to attend a wedding or a funeral. I think that all his life he associated the religious congregation and worship services with piety and self-righteousness. I can well remember his response to an event I told him about when, at the age of fourteen, I was working as assistant janitor at the Congregational Church. One Sunday, just before the service, it was discovered that the small room which contained the bread for Communion was locked, and the key could not be found. So one of the men on the vestry, a farmer of stern and severe temperament, used his considerable strength to smash the door in, shattering the frame and splitting the door casing. The janitor, Frank Stillwell, was disgusted by the gratuitous and exhibitionistic violence of that act, and so was my father. It prompted him to recall the hypocrisy of a number of supposedly devout, self-professed believers he had known. A story that sticks in my mind was of him and some of his boyhood friends snitching apples from the trees on the property of a parish house in Woodstock and being yelled at by the minister, who chased them away by throwing rocks at them, thus setting an odd example of Christian mercy in his casting of the first stone.

I have often wondered whether those early deaths in my father's family shook whatever religious beliefs he may have had early in his life, but I don't think he ever experienced anything like a full-blown crisis of faith. Like so much about him, whatever spiritual life he may have maintained he kept pretty much to himself. I remember hearing from my mother a story that seemed in keeping with his attitude toward organized religion. Once when he was visiting a tall, rangy, rough-natured old friend and former employee of the Woodstock Electric Company, who was hospitalized with leukemia at Dartmouth Hitchcock Hospital, his friend's wife entered the room and announced that the chaplain was wondering whether a little consultation might be in order. Whereupon her husband, from his bed, let her know in no uncertain terms that he wouldn't be needing any minister or priest under any circumstances, and he was greatly amused when my father, with a twinkle in his eye, said to her, "Your husband and I will say a little prayer here together." Evidently, the laugh they shared over the thought of the two of them, of all people, bowing their heads in supplication and reverence lifted his friend's spirits, as my father intended it to do. Though stoicism, as such, may not have been the belief of a great many men of that generation that had witnessed—either directly or indirectly in the horrors of two world wars separated by a great depression—suffering that would make their own experiences of adversity seem trivial, it was at least the posture they assumed. And I think they might have agreed with that character in one of Conrad's novels who says, "I believe in children praying—well, women too, but I rather think God expects men to be more self-reliant. I don't hold with a man everlastingly bothering the Almighty with his silly troubles." And yet, I suspect that in some way which he chose not to disclose, my father was a person of faith. My mother told me that not long before his death, she overheard him quietly saying the Lord's Prayer to himself there in his hospital bed, and she said she had long suspected that prayer was somehow an intimate aspect of his life. Did whatever faith he had experienced in his upbringing survive the devastation of 1923 and provide solace at that time, or did it desert him then and return when he discovered my mother and she delivered three healthy children and he saw therein a kind of grace like what Job experienced in the second family he came to love as he had loved the first family he had lost? There are no answers here. Like so much else about his life which he took silently to the grave, this dimension leaves us guessing, and he was essentially so much his own person that the questions themselves almost seem to me invasive.

Whatever his source of strength, my father showed considerable fortitude throughout his final illness and gave no sign of any fear of death. His primary concern was for my mother's well-being, and she told me that in the last months of his life he was worried about whether she would be able to manage on her own. She, of course, assured him that she would be all right, as she had many people she could depend on if she needed anything. Her sister Julia, herself a widow, came to stay with her for an extended period of time after my father's death, and her niece Mary Biathrow and Jane and her children often visited, and friends dropped in to see her. After Julia left, when Mother was for the first time alone in the house, at my suggestion she began reading Tolstoy's *War and Peace* and progressed through it slowly and deliberately, even studying the battle maps in the great Maude translation and rereading many passages she particularly admired. She reported regularly, in our telephone conversations, on her developing relationships with the Bolkhonskys and the Rostovs and Pierre Bezukhov and a host of others as she was coming to know them. And in the quiet of the house on Lincoln Street that late winter and early spring, with her cat for a constant companion, she lived so fully in nineteenth century Russia that she couldn't imagine what she would do when she reached the novel's end.

I now think it quite remarkable that my mother did as well as she did after my father's death. Throughout their life together, she had been devoted to him, putting his interests before her own, and adapting to what she saw as his wishes, and I think she aged considerably in his last years. Difficult as her life was without him, I know she took some consolation, as we all did, in having survived him, for he was in no way equipped to live without her. My experience of grief was, I suppose, not to be compared to hers, and yet there were some similarities. For both of us the moment of intense loss was delayed. Mother's occurred some weeks after my father's death when Julia was staying with her. Mine came most unexpectedly, very late in the winter. For two months after the funeral, my life was not so much painful as strangely dull and without much definition. I taught my classes, graded tests and essays, interacted with Maria and the children, conversed often with my mother on the phone, and called Howard and Jane from time to time to see how they were getting on, but there was a kind of darkness that wouldn't go away. During my spring break in early March, I made a solo trip to Woodstock to keep Mother company for a few days. One morning during this time, I awoke early, before daybreak, and, realizing I was not going to go back to sleep, got up and dressed, left Mother a note, and went out for a long walk. As I so often did, I went down Lincoln Street, crossed onto Bond Street, and entered the old neighborhood on Pleasant Street, then walked to Elm Street and went north toward the bridge and the north side of the Ottauquechee. I had no particular route in mind but soon found myself, as I often still do in dreams, wandering along the sidewalk that turns off the bridge away from the village, perhaps with the vague intention of circling around behind the mansion and coming out on North Street. The top of Billings Hill with its view eastward over the Billings Farm fields and the Ottauquechee River valley with Blake Hill in the distance, has always been, from early times when Howard and I were first taken there on Sunday outings with my parents, one of my favorite places in the world. On this particular overcast morning, winter was losing its grip. The ice had only just recently gone out of the river, which was riding high in its straight course down behind the buildings on lower Pleasant Street in the dull morning light that was beginning to brighten without any prospect yet of sunshine so that the fast-moving water was giving off glints of silver. And suddenly, in some mysterious way, my father was there with me, everywhere—next to me on the sidewalk and also in every aspect of the landscape at that moment—not as he had been in his illness, but long before that as he had been in my childhood: I felt the scrape of his whiskers as he hugged me goodnight, smelled his hair tonic, saw him mowing the lawn with the old hand mower down back of the house on Pleasant Street, and watching and sometimes assisting Howard and me as we were learning to ride our bicycles down behind Frost's Mill in Benson Place, and I heard his affected growling as he "tussled" with Howard and me in our pajamas. My gaze was directed across the fields and fixed on the river, and these clear images were all somehow dependent on the volume and velocity of the current which seemed impelled by some deep necessity to get beyond the valley it was sweeping through, and was flashing its own strange, compelling signals as it was carrying my father away from me. And without really understanding, I suddenly *knew* that he was, for his own reasons, departing; he had returned in one timeless moment for a kind of farewell on his journey to somewhere else. I gripped the top bar of the fence in front of me and strained forward to study the surface of the river when to my astonishment my chest heaved and I began to sob as I had not done since childhood. I was experiencing both a sense of loss and abandonment and a kind of awe at what I was seeing. After a short time, in some consternation and embarrassment over how I might appear to anyone passing behind me in a car along Route 12, I pulled myself together well enough to cross the road and walk the elevated section of lawn

down to the small Victorian summer house at the top of River
Street, also a frequent stop on our childhood walks, and got
myself in there largely out of sight and simply rode out, both as
mourner and as dazed spectator, what was happening to me.
And then I walked home.

William Maxwell says, "It is not true that the dead desert
the living. They go away for a short time, and then they come
back and stay for as long as they are needed. But sooner or
later a time comes when they are in the way . . . there is no
place for them in the lives of those they once meant everything
to. Then they go away for good." Though in my experience my
father has never gone away for good, in the thirty-six years
since that moment on Billings Hill I have never again sensed,
as I did then, his full presence. He was there at that moment to
let me know it was time to dispense with the thoughts of him
that had been weighing me down since his death and to move
ahead without him, and also to assure me that I would at odd
times be taken back the increasingly long distance to the days
of his life and meet some memory of him there. Whatever else
can be said of grief, it is perhaps best understood as the
survival of love beyond death, and as such, what first seems
too much to bear is ultimately what sees us through and
beyond it. It is in the calm and beneficent spirit of my father's
last visitation on that morning in March that I remember him,
and that spirit can be glimpsed only in one snapshot, the last
one, I believe, that was ever taken of him. Throughout his life,
he did not enjoy being photographed, and to anyone who knew
him, his expression recorded by the camera most often shows
at best a sort of thinly veiled patience, if not irritation, at having

been ambushed. My mother was much the same way, as can best be seen in a photo of them taken by a friend of mine one summer morning in 1964, when they were just coming out of the house to go to work. Evidently, the sight of the camera caught them by surprise, and their displeasure is obvious. It makes an interesting contrast to the last photo taken of them together some twenty years later in the last summer of my father's life. They are standing in the exact same place, on the back step, but unlike the earlier one which shows them in the flush of good health, in this later picture they are much thinner, my father wasted by emphysema and my mother pale and gaunt from her worry and concern over him. She is slightly turned away and looking down, perhaps at the small patch of irises she had planted next to the house, and he is leaning forward and resting the knuckles of his closed hands on the hood of the car in the posture that enabled him to breathe most easily. He is looking directly at the camera and uncharacteristically smiling in such a completely natural way that his face is wearing something like a beatific expression, as though he is saying "this is for posterity," and assuring us that his life, regardless of his early losses and his late suffering, had been accepted as a gift, and that life itself is not simply to be endured but to be honored and even blessed. No other photo of him resembles this last one, and its legacy has become indistinguishable from what I sensed moving along on the river's roiled and driven current in our last full experience together on that late winter morning on top of Billings Hill.

6. Legacy

I cannot imagine what my ongoing relation to my father might have been had I, like his brothers, elected not to marry and have children since so many of the ways in which I am and am not him have been realized in experiences with Maria and Lizzie and Jonathan. From the moment I was first informed by Maria in the winter of 1974 that she was carrying her first child, I gave little thought to what sort of father I was likely to be when the time came. That was nothing that could be prepared for; rather, it simply remained to be discovered. Only with the modern dissolution of family values have the artificial strategies of child rearing—subsumed under the ugly word "parenting"—substituted "roles" for natural filial relations and, in the process, increased the prevalence of dysfunctional families. Nevertheless, while I was waiting in awe for the appearance of my first child, I suppose I imagined I might be more like my mother than my father. Since in the Coffin family there were no uncles who had sired children, my other examples of fatherhood came from the men on my mother's side, beginning with her father, Hal Jillson, whom we adored. I may have set myself in some way to be like him, for from the time of my earliest relations with Lizzie and Jonathan, as I would be bouncing them on my knee or addressing them in all manner of silly affectionate diminutives or jigging them around the house in my arms to music on the radio or record player, I would suddenly recall moments with Grampa Jillson from my childhood. Uncle Gale, Julia's husband, was always as openly affectionate as my grandfather, and throughout his life would dispense hugs just as he had when we were children. Though my father had been openly affectionate with us when we were young, as we grew older he retreated somewhat to that distance between people which was most natural to him. My children took me back to my times with those men on my mother's side of the family. And I never assumed a greater physical distance from Lizzie and Jonathan as the years went by. My bubble is and always has been smaller than those of the men in the Coffin family.

However, such differences have not precluded discoveries of my father in myself, beginning with an unforgettable moment in 1977 when Maria and I and Lizzie were living in London and I was teaching at a school there. At the end of the school day, rather than depending on public transportation, I would walk the two miles or so eastward from Saint John's Wood to Primrose Hill and our apartment at 32 Chalcot Road. I chose to do so not so much for the exercise as for the peculiar sense of invigoration I receive from anonymity, from the sense of being something of a flaneur, alone and absolutely unknown in great cities, especially toward dusk when the lights begin going on in apartment buildings and office buildings. There I am, a moving and omniscient and silent witness among countless strangers going about their mysterious lives in such close proximity but at such great distance from me in a moment that belongs to us all as contemporaries. One particular winter afternoon, it was later than usual when I let myself in the front door and climbed the first flight of stairs to our second floor apartment. As I made the turn on the landing, I heard our door open above me and looked up the staircase to see Maria and the two-and-a-half-year-old Lizzie standing there; evidently, they had been waiting and listening for me. And I couldn't move. Suddenly, from being an all-seeing ghost and vicarious participant in the lives of strangers, I was my father in the mid 1940s coming home from work and being seen rounding the corner of the house by Howard and me peering out the glass in the door to catch sight of him. Right down to my green Harvard book bag, which suddenly became his green shopping bag, I was my father looking up the stairs at whom? At Lizzie, yes, but she was myself looking down the stairs at my father in such a way that my identity simultaneously dissolved and was enlarged by being at once the two generations that as child and father I was so mysteriously bringing together.

From that time forward, there have been similar experiences of transference in my relations with my children, but none that have so fully taken possession of me. They have occurred at moments when I was helping them in some way—to put together a Christmas present according to instructions or pump up a basketball or make an adjustment to a tricycle or bicycle or simply to tie their shoes—and my hands gripping the pump or wrench or screwdriver or shoelace suddenly belonged to my father, and I would remind myself to be patient. And it is true, as Jane was the first to point out to me, that I have his small hands, Howard's larger mitts coming from the Jillsons. But often enough it has been no physical resemblance or particular remark or event that would begin to blur the boundaries between my father and me and my children, but rather something emerging from the quiet times at home when Maria would be preparing supper and Lizzie and Jonathan and I would each be absorbed in our own activities. At such moments, when communication consists, in the words of William Maxwell, of "nods and silences . . . a tired curve of the mouth . . . a measuring glance over the top of the spectacles," when there is no need "to say what [you all] understand without its being said," the silence of rapport with its texture and residue of the unspoken, the tacitly understood, is felt to be timeless and is peculiarly susceptible to memory and a kind of dreaming. It harkens back to other lamp-lit rooms and my first family of parents and brother and sister, and so fully positions me there that, for the moment, my wife and children seem like unexpected guests, and these groupings in their shifting transmutations suggest something about the mystery of family life and the limits of what we can know about each other. Once again feeling myself to be both my father and my children, I hear myself speaking out of these blurred distinctions, almost involuntarily, against my father's own reticence and in opposition to the evanescence of it all, and saying something which to them may sound senseless, like, "Everything O.K.?" or "How are you folks doing?"—words that might translate simply to, "I'm here for you and open and available at this instant that is passing," something I can almost imagine my mother but not my father saying.

My mother often spoke with rapture of her childhood on the farm in South Pomfret, and my brother and sister and I feel a great attachment to our early years and delight in talking about them amongst ourselves and with our children. But my father seldom spoke about his childhood, for it was positioned as on the far side of the devastating events of 1923 and thus closed to him—except as a reminder of the fragility of family happiness—and to us as well. No doubt haunted all his life by those deprivations, he was and is to be found primarily in his adult life, where we discovered him and came to know him as well as we could. And given so much about him that was private, his life can be seen, with the help of memory, in the place where he lived it in its entirety. To many people of our cosmopolitan age, that life and the lives of his brothers might seem quaint and provincial: Chick, after the war, never venturing beyond New England; Ralph choosing to live in two towns only fourteen miles apart; Haze eventually leaving the village of Woodstock for his place in the country only eight miles to the north; and my father, except for some ten months in Boston in the '20s, living all his years within the village limits of Woodstock. So confined was that geographical space that he can be followed from birth to death on foot, without the use of an automobile, as I realized on what would have been his one-hundredth birthday on August 1, 2007. Being unable to make the trip from Connecticut to Woodstock, I decided to spend as much of that day as I could imagining myself there, retracing his old routes—out South Street to Vail field for Sunday afternoon legion team baseball games, along the north side of the park in the evening on his way with us to the Town Hall theater for the movies—until I had covered all the streets in the village as they were back then. But I kept coming back, as I have always done, to the short walk he made daily to and from work at the Woodstock Electric Company when we lived at 8

Pleasant Street. That is where he is to be found, on the east side of Elm Street, on his way home. And for some reason, that is where I come closest to what I imagine his inner life might have been. Wendell Berry has said that, "Living and working in the same place day after day, one is continually revising one's knowledge of it, continually being surprised by it and in error about it. And even if the place stayed the same, one would be getting older and growing in memory and experience, and would need for that reason alone to work from revision to revision. One knows one's place only within the limits and the limits are in one's mind, not in the place." To walk that familiar short distance in his footsteps is to sense a shift in vision and begin to catch the layered effect of so much time compressed into so little space, so that familiar stretches of sidewalk, storefronts in all weather, trees in their seasons, old houses, as well as being silent witnesses, become emblems, indexes, objective correlatives of thoughts and feelings as they occurred on site over a lifetime; as though each place in its present moment, like a painting glimpsed in a certain light, can reveal its pentimenti suddenly bleeding through and turning a then into a now. Such epiphanies may well have been the greatest returns on my father's investment in Woodstock. I suspect the village was, for him, inexhaustible.

Though I have resided elsewhere for more than half of my life, I've maintained a connection with Woodstock because it is still the place where I can live several different times of my life simultaneously and enjoy most fully the company of old friends and family and of those I have survived. In October of 1985, less than two years after my father's death, I made the trip from Connecticut to spend a weekend in Woodstock at foliage time. I arrived just in time on Friday afternoon to be taken off by Howard and Anya and my mother and sister on a hike up Mt. Tom to Pogue Hole, or "the Pogue," as we call it (a large pond in the woods) for a cookout. As darkness came on and we were sitting around our campfire, eating our supper and waiting for the moon to rise and gaze at itself in the water, and for the constellations to appear, Mother extended her wrist, looked at her watch, and said, to our surprise, "Well, forty-five years ago right at this time, your father and I were getting married—in Reverend Hines's apartment at 49 Central Street," which had long since been converted to office space. We had forgotten that it was Columbus Day, their anniversary, let alone that they were married at night, as she reminded us. There we were then, suspended between two times, so that moments later as I was stumbling around in the woods, collecting more firewood, I looked back and saw in the small, distant circle of firelight the dark forms and flickering faces of my family as they would have been had I not been there at all. I, as the absent one, was at that moment my father regarding us from the darkness. And later that night on our way home to Lincoln Street, Howard slowed the car as we were passing 49 Central Street to direct our attention to the darkened second floor windows, and said, "It looks as though the Reverend Hines, having performed the service and given his benediction to the newly-weds, has said his prayers and gone to bed."

Such time warps are part of my parents' legacy. The proximity of my mother and father since their passing is an intriguing aspect of my ongoing relations with them, particularly in the very different ways in which I sense their presence. My mother was entirely approachable, open and sympathetic. We had, I think, something like the same sensibility, the same curiosity and sense of wonder, the same interest in finding words for intimations and fleeting impressions. Her generosity of sentiment was such that to be with her anywhere was to gain the appropriate, full experience of each moment. Her presence had a way of revealing the inner radiance in things, lighting up the world. I can only suppose that she had the same effect on my father and helped to bring him out of the darkness. And I suppose these qualities were recognized by others. When it was decided by his family that Dr. Eastman, the beloved and highly respected physician who served Woodstock for so many years, needed someone to act as a part-time companion and chauffeur in his old age, he made it clear that there was only one person he would consider for that role, Arlene Coffin. Astonished but also honored by the request, my mother accepted the position, and over a number of years they greatly enjoyed each other's company and my mother came to know a great deal about the life of this otherwise very private man.

There are traces of her in all of us, her three children, and in her grandchildren as well. She is so strangely present in Lizzie that I find it hard to separate them. The thought of one brings with it the thought of the other and their two summers together in Woodstock when Lizzie was living with her at Lincoln Street—just the two of them—and working at a summer job in Gillingham's Store. Years after that when my mother was in a nursing home, suffering from dementia, she would still have her good days, and even some of her confusion showed her best qualities. Once, as I was visiting her, she asked me about her grandchildren, and I told her that, as a social worker in Chicago, Lizzie was working with foster children. Her instant response, was, "Oh, I want to do that." Suddenly, forgetting all about her immediate circumstances, she sounded and looked so young and perfectly lucid that my impulse was to say, "O.K., let's go," and take her out of there with the full confidence that if she were given the chance to serve the disadvantaged in any way, she herself would fully recover. But, coming to my senses, I thought to myself, "Mother, you already are doing it, because Lizzie's dedication to social justice comes from the depths of your humanity, and especially from your compassion for the unfortunate and the down-trodden; whether she is even aware of it, it's the two of you out there in the projects of the South Side, trying to make a difference." My mother's influence is diffuse and thus to be felt consistently in the world which received and returned her blessing. Her inner life overlapped with mine to shape the very character of my daily exchange with wherever I am in a way my father's did not. With him I felt the two of us to be discrete personalities. In his company it was so easy to feel effusive and invasive that I customarily withdrew somewhat and adopted something of his manner of self-containment to keep from encroaching on his space, hoping perhaps to win something of his approval by doing so. It was something like a persona I stepped into, the Coffin side of my nature I switched on. Perhaps it was these adjustments which have, at times, more often given me the sense of being him rather than of knowing him. In the company of Howard, my twin, who always seemed to me to be more natural around him, any silences in conversation that suggest something's remaining unspoken can suddenly make me feel that, simultaneously, I *am* my father and I am *sitting next to* my father. And it comes down into the next generation, in my son, in such a way as to suggest that my father is—to borrow a line from English novelist Edward C. Booth— "not dead in spirit, only changed in substance." For there is a kind of quietness or repose at the center of their being that skipped a generation in me, a thoughtful reluctance to deliver hasty post mortems, to pass judgement, in the interest of letting things reveal themselves in their own good time. In an ongoing kind of daydream, I imagine Jonathan and my father, who barely had any time at all together, encountering each other, entirely by chance, somewhere in Woodstock and instantly not only recognizing but also, quietly—without any drama or undue signs of excitement—understanding each other. I am always a silent witness to these meetings, looking on from a distance at their quiet communion, not interfering in any way, and willing to wait until Jonathan is ready to tell me what happened, what they said to each other, what lasting impression was made.

In the words of the poet Samuel Hazo, "The dead/possess us when they choose./The far stay nearer than we know/They are." "Nearer," indeed, in the case of my father, for, given the proverbial choice of climbing a thousand mountains or climbing one mountain a thousand times, he clearly opted for the latter. And its having been enacted in such a small space made it, I am sure, no less an adventure, for it included a great risk his brothers shied away from, that of investing himself, albeit under my mother's necessary encouragement, in a family in order to recover and perhaps redeem the first shattered one and, in the process, to resurrect something of the place, Woodstock, in which it was lost. And that place, Woodstock, was perhaps my father's greatest legacy to his children. As beneficiaries of it, we were fortunate, for I don't think many of our peers were given the same. Recently my sister was speaking about some of her classmates—people she was in school with from first grade through high school—and musing over how much and how little some of them were able to recall from those days. It occurred to me that the ones who came from the most materialistic and aspiring middle class families would quite likely have the weakest memories because their attention would always have been directed by their parents toward the life that had been designed for them that they were expected to fulfill, with their sights set on what they were supposed to become, thus making the present simply a time of effort, worry, and anticipation. And on that theory I had in mind two of her classmates who might be expected to have the least recall, the very ones, as it turned out, whom she went on to name. Never having been encouraged to give their attention to the here and now, but rather to fix it on the better life they were expected to work to achieve, they had lost their past; it had vanished because it had never been fully lived. By contrast to their parents, ours were grateful for the life they had been given and thus saw no need to wish for a better life for us. Working class as they were, they did not have the means and did not feel the need to ship us off to summer camp or to take us away on lengthy vacations, and, unlike some of the more well-to-do parents, they were not afraid simply to let us, unsupervised, be "townies" and fill our days with our own activities. They loved us for who we were, and they left us to ourselves so that from the time we were old enough to leave the house on foot or on our bikes, we were free, and our time was ours. We were out on our own, exploring the village in all seasons, giving it our full attention, watching it change each year as it took on the colors and shades of our developing inner lives, having our own experiences as we advanced from childhood to youth and adolescence and adulthood, glimpsing the inwardness of familiar things and building a treasure house of memory—in Edward Thomas's words, a "past hovering . . . ready to revisit the light"—and discovering for ourselves who we were and what we wanted to become.

I suppose my choosing to retain possession of the family home in Woodstock honors that legacy. A color photograph of Howard and me taken in the summer of 1989 when we were forty-seven shows us standing outside on the steps by the kitchen door with each of us holding one end of a banker's check that makes me sole owner of 43 Lincoln Street. Though we are not smiling, we are in accord. His decision to relinquish his share of the property took me by surprise. It was decisive and deliberate; he did not wish to be responsible for further maintenance and upkeep. My decision to buy him out was much less certain. He chose the moment while, in an odd way, the moment chose me. So much so that during the actual transaction itself, the irony of our role reversals—given our childhood experiences there, he should have been the inheritor—made me even more uncertain of my motives in buying him out. There were, of course, practical considerations which directed me: our parents had paid the taxes and taken care of the upkeep during their time there, and it seemed only right to keep it in the family as a place for my mother to live out the remaining years of her life. But beyond that, perhaps I was being guided by a lingering sense of summers spent there with my parents after Howard and Jane were married, and by the work I had put into the property during that time, scraping and painting the exterior of the house by myself. However, it was not until I was signing the deed that I was struck by something that made the experience seem somehow fated: when I wrote my middle name, which I seldom use, "Metcalf," I realized I was about to bring the house back entirely under the name of its original owner before my grandfather's alliance with that family eventually stamped it with the Coffin name. Were my decisions, uncertain as they had been, less mine than those of forces making use of me to accomplish their aims, which reached beyond my time?

Two recent events have drawn me closer to the old place. Ever since I can remember, an old, unstrung and damaged violin had resided in an antique wooden case in the attic. Since no one in the family, including my father and his brothers, knew anything about whom it had belonged to, or how it came to be there, its presence had always been a mystery. But Lizzie, in pursuit of an interest in bluegrass and old-time music, gave that violin an active place in the family by having it restored as her instrument on the way to becoming a good fiddler. And Jonathan asked if he and his wife Ilana and their infant daughter could spend an autumn weekend at the house. It made no difference to him, he said, that the place was for the time being almost completely unfurnished. They would simply put down on the dining room floor an inflatable king-sized air mattress, big enough for the three of them and their little black Patterdale Terrier, Lilly, and be right at home. That nativity, as it were, by which the fifth generation of the family was being brought into the old place, and the restoration of the old violin, entirely took possession of me—and I felt assured that my father would once again have been overwhelmed, as he was in his berry patch by the news of Lizzie's arrival on his sixty-seventh birthday. As for the house itself, some assurance of being in step with my ancestors has made the spirits of the place seem more benevolent to me than to my brother, who had been so at home there with Bertha but who recently informed some of my tenants that the place was haunted. That some shades of the past still reside there is probable, for the house is peculiarly resistant to change. It has taken on different characters in the arrangements and appointments of successive tenants, but its actual design and layout, with its many doors and its narrow hall spaces, has caused even confident interior designers I have consulted to throw up their hands in dismay at the impossibility of major renovations. Although we have made improvements, expenses incurred in the purchase of a second house have confined these changes to the kitchen and dining room, and, for the time being, have forestalled further alterations. As a result, the present, so to speak, exists primarily on the first floor, extending out to the porch, where what was once a grand pastoral view northward across the Ottauquechee valley and into the hills of Cloudland and Pomfret is now obscured by the growth of tall trees in the area that was always kept cut by our neighbors. To climb the stairs to the second floor, where the rooms have not been changed but simply been re-plastered and painted to lighten them, is to go back in time. And from there, to ascend the steep staircase to the third floor's unfinished attic is to enter the past. Not only does the dim, musty space in that largest of all rooms at the top of the house contain old foot lockers, wardrobes, and furniture from my grandparents' as well as my parents' time, but it also offers from its high north window, situated like a crows nest some seventy feet above the street below, the view we used to enjoy from the front porch so many years ago. Up there, still in the company of the bed where my grandmother slept when she was reduced to taking boarders in order to pay the taxes and keep the house, and in the presence of the antique Victrola and memorabilia from two world wars, it is impossible not to remember the world of my grandparents and to be drawn back to that first family who came to live in this house in 1927. Here, tucked away in trunks and desk drawers, are scraps and fragments of their world when they were all together, including a photo of Howard pushing a small wheelbarrow, which must have been taken not long before his death at age six. That it was never framed or even brought downstairs and was never shown to us by my father is part of that reticence about the lost son and brother that would have sealed him off from us had it not been for the letters to Haze from his family in 1922 and 1923. They show him to have been very much the object of his parents' affection, and he seems to have had a particular fondness for his oldest brother. Millie tells Haze, "Howard thinks quite a lot about you. He says he would like to go to Tilton and sneak into your room and surprise you someday." And "Howard talks about you often and wants to see you. He said the other night that he was your boy and wanted I should ask you what you were going to bring him for Christmas." As the youngest at that time, Howard seems to have had a special place in the hearts of all his older brothers. My mother told me that from the beginning of Millie's illness, my father was especially concerned about the well-being of his little brother and took it upon himself to look after him. And the eleven-year-old Chick may have felt the same way about him. In fact, the very few photos of Howard notwithstanding, it is a detail from a brief letter Chick wrote to Haze that gives me my most vivid and lasting image of him: "Howard has got a little lantern which he takes outside when it is dark." There he is, fixed in my mind's eye, standing on the lawn in a warm coat with winter coming on, his face encircled in the glow of his lantern as he peers into the darkness beyond a small area of illumination.

The disappearance of those two generations of the Coffin family has placed my grandparents almost beyond the reach of living memory. And my father and his brothers' reticence about their first home with their mother and their second home with their stepmother gives a special importance to my own early memories and to the artifacts discovered in the attic. Although my step-grandmother was more of a presence in our lives, it is to my grandfather that my thoughts most consistently return. Apart from a few photographs from his early years, there is the formal black and white portrait taken of him in his later years when he was married to Bertha and looking very much as I remember him. He is wearing a dark suit jacket over a white shirt and striped tie held in place with a tiepin, and is looking directly at the camera through round wire-rimmed glasses. He is a good-looking man, a gentleman. His face is that of someone who might easily be wounded but not quickly angered. His gray hair is neatly parted, and his expression suggests sensitivity and kindness. The epistolary Clarence Coffin, who was a more open person, full of pluck and good humor than the man I remember, is discernible in the hint of a smile and the suggestion of quiet amusement showing in his blue eyes and closed mouth. But he remains for me primarily as he was at those long ago family gatherings—pleasant but subdued and always in the background of the arrangements made by his second wife. His diaries, discovered in the attic at the bottom of a trunk, tell us little about him, for he recorded nothing of his thoughts and feelings, but simply spoke about business in Gillingham's Store—including stops on his delivery route—the weather, visits from family and friends, high school sports events, short trips taken on a weekend or a Thursday afternoon, when the stores were closed. But the entries which follow and extend the time covered by the letters into the latter half of 1923, do include more of his concerns about Millie's poor health. He records frequent house calls of two physicians, Dr. Eastman and Dr. Jackson, as well as a period of confinement in Mary Hitchcock Hospital in Hanover and finally a time in Randolph sanatorium to give premature birth to Ralph in June. From that time forward, the story is one of her decline and finally her death on October 7, less than a month after

Howard's. The diary entry simply states, "Millie passed away @ 8:45 in a convulsion." It is written in the same steady hand that recorded the information about Howard's death on September 12: "Little Howard collided with an auto [in] front [of] J. S. Brownells. Skull fractured taken to Hanover Hospital & died at 6 p.m. not regaining consciousness. Warren G[illingham] with [me] to the end brought me home." I have asked myself whether that steadiness suggests a realization and acceptance of the fact that the life he was evidently born for was asking of him an almost unimaginable kind of fortitude. In his attempt to reassure Haze that he would be able to manage what was required of him during Millie's last months and to dissuade him from dropping out of school to assist him, he writes, "I can hoe my row, another if I have to and also carry an extra hoe on my back." And it is possible that he had discovered in himself this fortitude in the days following Howard's death and burial. Still, I picture him by himself on the night of September 12, about to close his diary, sitting in stunned awe that he could have made his notations for the previous day without some intimation of what would be required of him when he next picked up his pencil and opened that small book with its dated and lined pages. Before he retired for the night, did he sit there in the lamplight for an immeasurably long moment in disbelief at what he had just written until the words themselves seemed to be regarding him in astonishment that he was still living? Being a father myself, I cannot imagine the depth of his grief. And beyond the sense of loss, did he blame himself for Howard's death? Among the articles put away in the attic and discovered long after my grandfather's lifetime is a small black and white snapshot showing him sitting by himself on the Gillingham delivery wagon. He is wearing a dark suit and flat cap and is holding in one hand the reins of the horse, with the other hand resting on his knee, and he is looking at, or in the direction of, the photographer. The picture is taken from the sidewalk on the south side of lower Pleasant Street, looking across the street to the Brownell house, and so, by design or by chance, it captures the exact place where his son was killed. The photo is undated, but it is impossible to look at it very long without seeing it through my grandfather's eyes. If it predates the fatal accident, then to him its record of both the place where Howard was struck by the car and the house to which his unconscious body was carried must have represented the fragility of their happiness in the time before the fatal illness of his wife made it necessary for him to take his son with him on the delivery route—a time of family safety and security before they were all visited by what the Vermont Standard referred to as "those misfortunes of ill health and accident that have seemed to dwell with them persistently in the past few years." But if the photo dates from the years following the misfortunes, then for my grandfather its most blinding detail might have been the empty place next to him on the seat of the wagon as the spot where he had last seen and spoken to the small, blond boy before leaving him unattended in order to disappear momentarily into the house across the street, rather than—and here the mind reels before the vivid and perfectly possible alternative—telling him to come along with him and, by so doing, saving him from the inconceivable disaster. If and for how long the quiet, elderly man I knew carried with him such agonizing images and thoughts, I don't know; that he was not entirely broken by them and by the death of his wife, which followed soon after the death of his son, is, I suppose, a testimony to such inner strength as he could muster to pick up the pieces of his shattered life and carry on.

I don't remember the last time I saw my Grandfather Coffin. From time to time after my grandmother's death and our move to Lincoln Street, we would go with my father to visit him on Pleasant Street, where he had taken a room and was given his meals at the home of a Miss Kathryn Gates, a kindly woman who took in guests and resident boarders. During these visits, Howard and I would fill him in on how we were doing in school and what sports we were playing, and would fidget as we listened to my father, who also seemed at some loss for words, filling him in on Jane, saying what little there was to say about Haze or Chick or Ralph, and mentioning some events in Woodstock. I can well imagine that their conversation was much the same when Howard and I were not there with them—so much of the personal and of the past going unspoken. In good weather Grampa Coffin was to be seen out walking in his three piece suit and hat and with his cane, and he would often join the old men on the side steps of the Corner Fruit Store to study and assess the present life of the village, which had by that time largely passed them by, and to swap stories and talk of better days. He was even more inaccessible than his sons, and, being young and knowing much less than I do now about the hardships and losses he experienced, I regret to say I felt no desire to know him better. But while his imagined suffering in one way takes me closer to him, in sympathy at least, it also sets him off at an unapproachable distance. The bonds of compassion are indissoluble, but those people who are strangely called upon to endure what seems more than their share of adversity seem set apart from us on some "sad height" beyond the reach of our empathy and our words. And I can well imagine that, were I to come before him once again, I would be all but silenced and brought up short of all feeling except a kind of awe, less apt to speak than to bow.

If, as I suspect, something in my grandfather and his sons never fully recovered from these losses, then what might be seen as Bertha's unsuitability for the roles of second wife and stepmother seems mitigated by the difficulty of the task she took on. And as much as she may, even with the best of intentions, have mismanaged her new place in the Coffin family, or, more accurately, their place in her house, I can appreciate and fully sympathize with her desire to help them and, in the process, to achieve some measure of family happiness herself. My last and in some ways most indelible memory of her, before she was stricken with cancer and I hardly saw her at all, comes from our apartment on Pleasant Street, probably not more than two years before her death in 1957. I came home from school one autumn afternoon to discover her seated at the kitchen table, talking with my mother. Surprised to see her, I for some reason said, in a proper British accent, "Well, if it isn't Grandmother Coffin!" and then wondered if I had sounded foolish or rude in doing so, only to be reassured by their laughter and their answering me in kind, and I gave her my hand. It occurs to me now, as I think it did then, that I was old enough so that she seemed less judgmental and disapproving than I had found her to be in my childhood. After we had talked for a while and she rose and pinned on her hat and put on her coat and was bidding us goodbye, I realized she was there as much with hopes of seeing her grandchildren as of visiting with my mother. Moments later, after she had left, I looked out the kitchen window and saw her making her way eastward along the sidewalk of the bridge over the Kedron. She was stooped somewhat, carrying her shopping bag and hand bag and walking slowly, and in a way that had never happened before, my heart went out to her. I don't remember where she was bound, but I surprise myself even now, with how insistently I try to think she was walking only as far as the post office where she had arranged to meet Uncle Jim and catch a ride with him as he got off from work, and was not setting out on the long trek from the center of the village up to Lincoln Street by herself.

For the most part, the dead offer us no second chances. Whatever their purpose may be for visiting us in dreams, it is not to help us fill in the pieces of their lives we seek after they have departed. For they arrive as though from a long way off, and, strangely, though we recognize them instantly, something slightly alien about them discourages an easy familiarity. We feel constrained by something more than the boundaries of our earthly relations with them, of which we are reminded by their faces in the photographs that preserve them and keep them among us. But with Millie, my father's mother, the case is different, for we never saw her, never knew her; she is heard by us only as she is speaking about them all—her husband and her three sons—in the letters to James Hazen, her first-born, and she was almost never spoken of by any of them. Other than that, her photographs show us, at least at first glimpse, the face of a stranger. She is to be seen most clearly in two that have come down to us from her early life. In one, taken on July 4, 1895, when she was sixteen, she is seated in an open carriage beside her mother and across from two other ladies. In front of them are two men in white shirtsleeves and dark trousers and vests and bow ties, one of whom is holding the reins of the two horses. The women are dressed in long skirts, and their hair is done up and pinned under jaunty straw hats perched on top of their heads. Millie is leaning back against the seat, arms folded, and looking straight ahead with a kind of smirk, suggesting impatient expectation. My brother, who, with my mother's assistance, labeled this and a number of old photos, has written on the back, "Mother sees Millie as 'slouched down, waiting to have some fun.'" It is something straight out of the gay nineties. But the other photo, which was discovered in the attic years after the death of her husband and all her sons, brings her directly to us from more than a century ago, as a young woman. It is an oval black and white picture in which she is positioned at an oblique angle with her head turned toward the camera, and she is looking slightly toward the right. And whereas the other pictures of her are period pieces, suggesting something of the time in which they were taken, this one could have been taken yesterday. Her shoulders and neck are bare, as is the upper part of her chest down to the dark edge of her low-cut dress or robe; she is wearing no necklace, and her heavy brown hair, which catches the light, is swept away from her forehead and ears. Her features have something classic about them with her perfectly shaped aquiline nose and chiseled, full lips, but what is most extraordinary is her large blue eyes. There is nothing shy or demure there, nor is there a hint of vanity or boldness, but rather a look of complete candor and a suggestion of amusement, of good humor. There is also no evidence of self-consciousness in front of the camera; in fact, the expression is such that the person she is regarding with her full attention might momentarily feel exposed and look away. It is as though she is saying, "This is who I am," and though she might not know it or think it important, she is quite lovely. In a book on his adventures as a biographer, Richard Holmes qualifies the idea that, "In a photograph . . . 'an instant of time is frozen' like a bucket of water taken from a flowing river or a tableau held in a theatrical production," by contending that some photographs establish "a continuity of time, a linking of one 'instant' to the next across many years, with a dissolving (rather than a freezing) of much that was temporary and ephemeral." Indeed, Mildred Anthony is seen by us here not as fixed in some past moment but as eclipsing all the years between the minute when the photographer disappeared under his black cloth to snap the picture and the ongoing present when she is simply here before us, the descendants she never knew. And this continuity is underscored by the presence of so many of her children and even of her grandchildren in her face. I was once invited to a reunion of the Frost family, courtesy of Robert Frost's granddaughter Lesley Francis. When I walked into the room where the event was being held, I was struck by the way all of the three generations gathered there resembled the poet even though in many cases they did not look much like each other. It was as though the ancestor and progenitor had printed off a limitless number of variations on a theme. In the case of my father's family, if Uncle Jim most closely resembles his father in looks, his three brothers look at me from their mother's face simultaneously and in succession, beginning with my father, as I approach Millie's portrait from across the room, and suddenly switching to Ralph up close, and then to Chick. The shape of her face is theirs, as are her nose and eyes and, in the case of my father, her forehead. And it is with some astonishment that I recognize what my sister insists is the exact resemblance between her lips and mine; then suddenly there is Jane's face looking at me from the oval frame in an expression I have seen many times when she is listening to me and is about to give back as good as she gets by handing me a page from my own book. And then I catch a hint of Lizzie in her forehead, and of Jonathan in her large eyes. Had she lived to see the arrival of the next generation, she certainly would have understood my brother and me, two more boys added to the five she bore, and how delighted she would have been at the arrival of Jane, a girl in the family at last! Since my father was not one to complain, even in his last days, and I cannot recall his ever expressing regrets about the life he had been given, there is a special poignancy and even pathos in my mother's recollection of his telling her, as he did many times throughout their years together, "I wish you could have known my mother." If he never said as much to us, his children, it was no doubt because he did not want us to think he was recommending her over Bertha, the only Coffin grandmother we ever knew. But from the time he himself first had children, his experience as a father must have been tinged with heartache at the way his mother's early death prevented us from having any time with her at all and prevented her from coming to know us. And for me that early departure raises the question that has shadowed the entire search that prompted this inquiry: who would my father and his brothers have been had she lived at least as long as her husband, my grandfather, and who would we have been? How would the lives of her grandchildren been shaped by her presence? For the face that looks out from its oval portrait with such disarming honesty in its appetite for life convinces one that she would have left her mark on anyone fortunate enough to have known her and to have been loved by her.

If, when I was young, I thought about my father and my uncles' early years with their mother, I suppose I assumed that their reticence was the result of their childhood and youth's having occurred so long ago, as though in my inability to imagine those grown men as boys it was natural to think that they themselves had forgotten those times. But, as I realized much later in life, those are the times which are never forgotten. Though I have always idealized and delighted in recalling my own childhood, it was not until I was in my early fifties and my children were in their teens that I found my lifeline had left the horizontal and curved around so I suddenly seemed to be standing closer to my early years than ever before and looking directly across into them with such clarity of recall as to inspire a book about that experience. And it taught me as never before the truth of something I recalled from Robert Louis Stevenson:

"We advance in years somewhat in the manner of an invading army in a barren land; the age that we have reached . . . we but hold with an outpost, and still keep our communications with the extreme rear and first beginnings of the march. There is our true base; that is not only the beginning, but the perennial spring of our faculties." If my father and his brothers' experience was in any way like mine—and I assume my father's being a father himself would have made it so—then their years, as they accumulated, must have taken them back again and again, however great the cost in sorrow, astonishingly close to their mother as they had known her. And if so, I can only interpret the silence with which they kept her in their hearts as an expression of her full and continuing presence in their lives time without end, and as the source of so much about them that could not be known.

Claustrophobia

A few years ago, my son and I went into the Naples Pizza in New Haven for lunch. After we were seated, I excused myself to visit the men's room, which I remembered was in the basement. I went out into and across the first dining area and down the stairs and along the narrow corridor to the room in the back, a cramped space which was just big enough for a toilet and sink. I slid the bolt to lock the door, and a few moments later, the lights suddenly went out in the room and in the corridor outside. It was pitch black, and I have a bad time with tight spaces, even when they are well lighted. In some alarm, I began running my hand up and down the doorframe to unlock the door, but I could not find the bolt. After several tries, I was concentrating on not panicking, telling myself over and over that the bolt had to be there. I was still rational enough to realize that if I lost control and tried to break down the door, I could jam the lock or injure my shoulder and be in a worse situation. Finally, after what seemed a very long time, and after many slow tries in the complete blackness, I found the bolt, slipped it, let myself out into the utter darkness of the hallway, and groped my way to the bottom of the curved stairs, from the top of which I could see a bit of light. When I got up to the restaurant, I asked the woman behind the counter if she had just switched off the basement lights, and she said she had, and I told her what a situation she had put me in by doing so.

"What were you doing down there?" she asked.

"Using the men's room," I answered.

"Oh, no," she said, "that's up here, out across the way."

"Not the last time I was here," I answered.

We then realized that I had visited the discontinued men's room, and she was very apologetic. And at that moment, my claustrophobia took on an even more frightening dimension: if I had not been able to get out of that room in that abandoned part of the building, my son would never have known where to look for me. He had not seen which way I turned after I left the table, and, as I discovered, he, being a frequenter of the restaurant, knew about the men's room on the main floor but nothing whatsoever about the one in the basement.

If claustrophobia such as that I suffer from can be inherited, then I certainly know how it came to me, and to my brother and sister, and that is through my mother. She was the most claustrophobic person I have ever met, and it's really her story that needs to be told.

When she was in her 70s and suffering some health problems, she was strongly advised to undergo a series of tests in an MRI, which is short for magnetic resonance imaging. It is an extraordinary piece of medical technology which puts people in a magnetic field that rearranges the nucleus of the cells by sending in a radio signal. The end result is a series of miniature images of the brain, something like x-rays but far more sophisticated. The tests require the person being examined to lie completely enclosed and motionless in a very small area inside the machine.

Even for people who have no problem with cramped spaces, the MRI can be a pretty trying experience. And for anyone who is at all claustrophobic, it is a nightmare. Fortunately, there is now such a thing as an open MRI, though it offers only two narrow and distant peripheral views outside the enclosure. So about the only way for any claustrophobe to get through the tests, short of being completely anesthetized, is the way an old friend of mine chose a few years ago: he got so juiced on tranquilizers that, as he put it, he would have experienced euphoria in an oubliette. But that way was not open to my mother because she was violently allergic to all painkillers and tranquilizers.

Clearly, she had to come up with another plan, and she did, and it was this. So as never to set eyes on the outside or the inside of the MRI, she would wear a blindfold during the entire time of the test. The problem was that for anyone as claustrophobic as she, blindfolds can be pretty frightening, so what was she to do? Well, she decided that the only way to prevent total panic from occurring inside the double enclosure of blindfold and machine would be to create a world in her mind's eye and to be out there in that world for the duration of her ordeal. She would take an imaginary walk, a five mile stroll from her house in Woodstock, Vermont out into the countryside and back into the hills and valleys of Pomfret to the farm where she was born and where she spent the first eighteen years of her life with her parents and four of her five brothers and sisters. To her and to all our family, and even to people seeing it for the first time, that farm in its setting is one of the most beautiful places in the world.

With the understanding that the MRI test might take as long as an hour, my mother set about organizing and rehearsing her journey. She had a month in which to prepare. It was winter, and since my father had died a few years before this time, she was alone in the house. During that month, for over one hour every afternoon, she would take the phone off the hook and tie a bandanna around her head, covering her eyes, and lie down on the couch, and, in her imagination, walk from there, the house of her old age in the 1990s, back to the home of her childhood in the 1920s. She didn't have to be taken out in the car to refresh her memory because she had spent her entire life in Woodstock and Pomfret and knew every step of the way, every house and roadside tree, every curve of the brooks that the roads follow and pass over, and all the places where the different kinds of wildflowers could be found. And besides, a trip in the car would only put her that much more in touch with winter, and she had decided to take her long walk in the spring. Throughout her entire time in the MRI, she was going to be in another season, and in another time as well as another place.

She was making progress in her rehearsals, she told me. She was avoiding the center of Woodstock by cutting through Bond Street and going past the house on Pleasant Street where we had lived when my brother and sister and I were children; she was enjoying as always the great houses along Elm Street, the view eastward from Billings Hill out over the fields and across the Ottauquechee River, and relishing that exhilarating feeling of reaching the village limits and really being on her way, and the weather on her May morning was, she was pleased to report, just perfect. I began to picture her lying there on the couch. There would certainly have been few distractions. Outside, snow fell; inside the house, the only sounds were those of the furnace doing its job against the January cold and an occasional bump as a chickadee settled on or lifted off the bird feeder on the porch, and the muffled, thunderous purring of her enormous white cat, Fred, curled up at her feet. If her plan worked on the day of the test, she would have accomplished a small triumph of memory and imagination over what would have been for her nothing much less than a kind of living entombment in the MRI.

When the month was up and the day of the test came around, my sister drove her to the Dartmouth Hitchcock Medical Center in Hanover, New Hampshire. Mother felt prepared, but so as not to take any chances, she put on her blindfold in the radiology waiting room. When the time came for the test, my sister Jane led her blindfolded to the MRI, at the sight of which Jane nearly succumbed to an attack of vicarious panic. But, doing a wonderful job of acting, she managed to conceal her fright by sounding cheerful as she stood by to see the medical technician close Mother into the machine.

The test took the better part of an hour. I phoned Mother that night to ask her how it all went.

"Fine," she said. "It was all right."

"Did you keep your blindfold on?" I asked.

"Oh, yes, I certainly did!" she assured me.

"And you took your walk to the farm?"

"Well, yes," she said hesitantly, "but I didn't get there."

"You didn't?" I asked in some surprise. "Why not, did you walk too slowly?"

"No, I was going along fine until I got just past the Conklin farm [which is probably a little less than half way], and I looked up the road and saw the old Harding place with the attached barn sagging and the paint just peeling off the house. I had forgotten how the current owners have just let that place go. Why, I can remember when Oscar Harding had it and then George Nelson after him—you know it was in that family for generations—and it was such a nice place, even later when Ward Canaday had it in the 40s and early 50s. But ever since the new people have lived there—since when? probably the mid 60s—it has just looked worse and worse. I was so annoyed that I could not bring myself to walk past it and see it that way. So that is as far as I got in my walk. I had to stop right there."

Astonished, amused, sympathetic, I asked, "But you didn't see that in your rehearsals? You didn't remember the way the house looks when you were prepping for your trip?"

"Evidently not," she said.

"Maybe because those were just rehearsals," I suggested.

"Yes, I thought of that too," she answered.

"Well, then Mother, how did you get through your time in the MRI if you couldn't complete your walk? I was worried that if there were any hitches or interruptions, you'd be in for an awful time."

"I don't know," she said. "I thought of you children some, and my grandchildren. It wasn't bad. I don't know."

And that is where she left it and where she left us. And I have never stopped asking myself what happened to her there under her blindfold in that machine. The strange fact of her suddenly seeing the old Harding place as it was right then and not as she had been picturing it in her practice sessions at home on the couch would not let go of me. It was easy enough to imagine that most of the details of the walk from Lincoln Street to the farm on Bartlett Brook Road in South Pomfret would have been those from her early life since they are the ones stored longest and most deeply imprinted in memory, as I knew from my own experience. Solo trips from Connecticut back to my hometown of Woodstock are spent largely in anticipation of seeing the village in which I grew up, no matter how many times upon arrival I have been assaulted by the sight of missing or gentrified buildings and strangers drifting about looking like imposters. However, the rude shock that my mother experienced came not from a direct confrontation that corrected memory but from a revision of memory she was completely unprepared for by all her rehearsals, in which she had done her best to replicate the situation she would find herself in on the day of her test: her supine position on the couch which substituted for the interior of the machine and the same blindfold worn in both places. Could it be that an unavoidable measure of anxiety at being in the hospital and facing the situation and at hearing the noise of the MRI performing its task—things that she had not been able to imagine—somehow opened in her mind the capacity to be surprised and allowed her to be present to what was beyond her control in a way she had not been during all of her sessions spent preparing herself? The Harding place, then, suddenly appeared to her in its current semi-derelict state, something she had unconsciously suppressed in walking past it in her mind's eye. Something incomplete in her possession of the past had left room for the unexpected. Or she may have been assuming an ability to control time that is simply beyond human capacity. Her plan was to prepare for a dreaded future moment and to survive it by reaching into the past for an old familiar journey that would take her out of her immediate present surroundings altogether for the time required. The surprise was a kind of ambush suggesting that in any lived human moment, even one in which the present is flooded by recollection, contingency cannot be eliminated. We can plan for the journey, but we cannot control it, and we certainly cannot control our thoughts along the way. Suddenly, there was that house with its peeling paint, unkempt lawn, unused front door without steps, and sagging barn, demanding a response of some sort. Perhaps she got through the tests without claustrophobia not so much in spite of, as *because of,* her sense of outrage at the neglectful management of that property. I can imagine that she could have whiled away quite a few minutes in thinking of what the owners ought to be told about that old place as it once was and still should be. In some ways righteous indignation is a tonic, a real energizer, the other side, maybe, of reverence. But I don't think it was indignation as such that saved her in that hour. Rather, it was her deep and abiding sense of her destination, her childhood home, the memory of which, we know, was never very far from her thoughts. So much so that whether or not she actually arrived there at her destination that day, she had repeatedly reached it in her travels on the couch, and it was always with her as a kind of beacon and as a source of gratitude and joy and hope throughout her entire life, especially as she got older, as though that farm in Pomfret were not so much something left behind as it was a place out there ahead of her where the end might someday touch the beginning.

These are some of my thoughts about the strange way in which my mother's long imaginary walk was interrupted and how she could have survived her ordeal. To me they sound a bit didactic and strained and, finally, unsatisfactory. What happened there still speaks more loudly than what can be said to answer the questions it raises. Or, as the poet Stanley Plumly states it, "Exposition is the enemy, or at least too noisy, like tin cans tied to the tail of the experience." And, in some way, I know that; I have come to understand that when I consider and try to explain her strange experience, I do so mostly to watch my ideas fall short and fail in the face of some elusive truth that I seem to be catching the drift of in the story of my mother and the MRI and the imaginary journey she arranged to take. "I don't know," my mother said with some wonder about what happened to her. And *I* don't know either. She has been gone for twenty years now (she died in January of 2000), and so in some ways the story takes us as close as we will ever get to who she was, and very close as well to all that we didn't know about her and may never know. In the case of loved ones, in death as in life, we are intimately aware at once of both their continuing and abiding presence and also their distance and inaccessibility. My siblings and my wife and children and I feel ourselves to be very much in touch with my mother when we are telling and pondering this story in which the planned narrative was so unexpectedly interrupted, leaving us baulked in expectation and requiring us all to abandon what we thought should happen for what might and did happen instead. She left us something beguilingly unfinished that would keep her here before us and remind us that we experience some of our clearest and deepest moments of insight and comprehension not from certainty but from the enlargement of vision that arises in the presence of mystery. Mystery, in Eva Brann's words, "not as an intellectual conversation stopper, but an ever-compelling perplexity that is not resolved just by being increasingly clarified." In this story of my mother and the MRI, it is the mystery of human individuality and the strangeness of the world in which we continually discover our lives to be taking place.

Al Powers

*There's no rock bottom to the life. He's a man way
out there in the blue, riding on a smile and a shoeshine.... A salesman is got to dream, boy. It comes
with the territory.* — ARTHUR MILLER

For many years Al Powers was often to be seen walking
along lower Central Street in Woodstock, Vermont in a
self-absorbed way, carrying a briefcase and talking to
himself. He was a tall, thin man in late middle to early
old age who somewhat resembled both George Raft and Basil
Rathbone, and his manner of dress caught one's attention: in
the summer he wore loose-fitting light colored slacks or—
something we seldom saw on a man of his age—Bermuda
shorts with long dress socks and hushpuppies and sport shirts
always buttoned at the top. He gave little thought to matching
attire, and, though he sometimes got it right, his color combinations and clashing patterns of plaids and stripes could be
startling. He looked like a person one would meet at a resort
hotel in Florida, who had suddenly been transplanted to the
streets of a small New England town. Though he walked as
though something was very much on his mind, he would

happily pass the time of day with anyone who spoke to him or happened to catch his eye. I had known Al by sight for years by the time I was first introduced to him in the early 60s when my brother Howard was working summers as bellhop captain at the old Woodstock Inn and Al had a job there at the main desk as night clerk. They had the Red Sox in common, and Howard had been invited to dinner a couple of times at his and his wife Inez's house, and came away raving about her spaghetti. Al and Inez were actually neighbors of ours on Lincoln Street in Woodstock, their house at #25 being just a ways down the hill from ours.

Al had the reputation of being a kind of local character. At almost any time of year, he could be seen going in and out of stores and various places of business as a sort of traveling salesman, peddling the wares of the Newton Manufacturing Company of Newton, Iowa, which specialized in promotional products, and he carried a briefcase stuffed with samples. As he did not drive (I seem to recall something about an accident when he was young and was first learning, though I'm not sure why he never had a license), he did most of his business in Woodstock and some of its neighboring towns like Hanover, Lebanon and White River Junction, which he would visit by catching a ride with people who commuted daily to those places. He was well known to most of the merchants, who were, at times, somewhat less than thrilled to see him coming through their doors. Al could be a talker, and once he was started on his sales pitch, you understood pretty quickly that he'd be there for a while. He had the salesman's manner of addressing you repeatedly by your first name, but for some reason when he was looking you in the eye, his gaze seemed to settle on your forehead. Up onto the counter would go his briefcase, and out of it would come brochures and samples—of lapel pins, note pads, golf tees, pencils and pens, magnetic clips, matchbooks, key tags, lip balm, pen spray sanitizers, zip purses, mini round tape measures—all, of course to be inscribed with the name and advertising slogan and address of your business—and for a time, an item that was one of his specialties: Brite View Cleaners, a pocket eyeglasses cleaner that came in a small, Chapstick-looking tube. Al would introduce it, give his spiel, and then ask you for your glasses (I don't *think* he simply took them off your face), smear the clear stuff on both sides of the lenses, and then wipe them off in a very deliberate manner with a clean handkerchief he carried in his pocket for that purpose. For a time, we had quite a few of these tubes lying around the house because they actually served their purpose quite admirably and because my parents and my brother and sister and I were very fond of him and tried to support him in his endeavors. Though I sometimes heard storekeepers say they quickly ordered a product or two just to be rid of him, most people liked Al and treated him with a kind of bemused tolerance. I remember once ordering a pair of cordovans from Shurtleff's Store in Woodstock when I was living in New Jersey. When the package arrived and I unwrapped it and cut the tight string around the box, out spilled dozens and dozens of floppy plastic shoehorns bearing the name and phone number of the store (courtesy of the Newton Manufacturing Company); they had been crammed into every available space in the box and stuffed into both shoes by my friend Dave Doubleday, who worked for his father, a regular customer of Al's, and found it necessary at times to clean house of his purchases.

Al had a style all his own. He was not a native Vermonter and didn't talk like one, but hailed from Beverly, Massachusetts and had retained a slight trace of the North Shore accent. And he was something of a city slicker. Born in 1897, he had first come to Woodstock as a youth in the early years of the century to visit his grandparents, who lived on South Street in one of the white frame houses that were demolished to make room for the current Woodstock Inn. After high school in Beverly, he graduated from Baypath Institute in Massachusetts, served in the army during World War I, and then was enrolled briefly in law school at the University of Virginia in the late 1920s before he began a career of working at various hotels including the Hotel Coolidge in White River Junction and the prestigious Greenbriar Hotel in White Sulphur Springs, West Virginia. He also worked as manager of the Allison Hotel in St. Petersburg, Florida and of the Worthy Inn in Manchester, Vermont in the 1940s. He had a kind of dapper quality in spite of his some-times odd getups, and one could easily imagine him in spats and a tux or in the summer weight suits and ties he still some-times wore, greeting guests in the lobbies of the big hotels of the 30s and 40s. He smoked cigars and liked the good life. Every summer he managed to get in a few rounds of golf at The Woodstock Country Club with some of his men friends from town, though he was, as he confessed, a very average golfer. I remember him telling my father that he never in his life broke 80, though he "once came damned close." He was, as he recalled it, on the 18th green, lining up a dead certain three-foot putt, when one of his partners made the mistake of asking another—who was keeping score—"How's Al, doing, anyways?" The answer, "78," so unnerved him that he choked and, in his own words, "hit one of [his] best drives ever," overshooting the hole in such fashion as to require several strokes before he could finish, and he maintained all his life that if those guys had kept their mouths shut, he'd have managed a 79 for sure.

Though he was never one to boast, I inferred from a few things he said that he had been something of a ladies' man in his day and had not passed up certain opportunities for romance offered by hotel employment. Inez was his third wife. About his first two marriages I know very little. The first one evidently took place in Virginia during or right after his law school days, or when he was working at the Greenbriar. From what Al told me, he didn't remember much about it. He was out in the backcountry somewhere on a lark with a few friends, and, as he put it, "Somebody dug up a pumpkin, we got into the moonshine, and when I came to a few days later, I was married." That was about all he ever said on the subject. Evidently, though the marriage was short-lived, it did last long enough to produce a daughter. His second marriage was to a Woodstock girl, Violet (Wilson) Makepeace, who later married my father's brother Chick and became my Aunt Vi. Violet had been well brought up and was fashionable and had gone to Katharine Gibbs School in Boston or New York. She also liked men and liked to drink and have a good time. I think in one way or another she was too much for Al, or he was not enough for her, but in their time, which was short, the two of them must have made quite a dashing couple.

His third wife, Inez (Watkins) Clancy, was a Woodstock girl. For a time after graduating from high school in 1922, she lived and worked in New York City. During those years she married an Irishman named Clancy, and they had a daughter, Jean. After the marriage dissolved, she and her daughter moved back to Woodstock, and settled into the family home on Lincoln Street, and Inez worked as a bookkeeper, first at Costello's Garage on Cross Street and then at A&B Motors on South Street. But I first remember her as the very pretty, prematurely gray-haired lady who sat up on the high stool behind the glass of the ticket booth in the Woodstock Town Hall Theatre and sold us our tickets for the Saturday afternoon matinees. She and Al married on October 12, 1948, and Al came to live at her home in Woodstock. Neither of them saw a great deal of their children or grandchildren. Inez's daughter, who was a divorcee, visited them once a year or so for a short time, and Al's daughter, a happily married and attractive woman with two well adjusted children, would stop by with her husband in the summer or early fall on their trips to New England in their camper. Though she and Al got on very well and were always very happy to see each other, they must have been out of touch during her childhood and youth. In fact, as Inez told us a number of times, still in some disbelief, she did not even know Al was a father until they were out for dinner on their tenth anniversary and he said, "Honey, I've got something to tell you: I've got a daughter named Jean, same as you."

The house where Al and Inez lived on Lincoln Street was a large, imposing old two-storied structure with a barn attached. It sat on a few acres of land at the top of a curved driveway well above the street, and it was situated so as to offer a grand view northward out over the Ottauquechee valley. On both sides of the house and sloping upwards in the back were fields of long grass which they kept clear, and it was one of the common sights of summer to see Inez's brother Elmer out there in his overalls and blue work shirt swinging his scythe until the job was done. He was afflicted with Sydenham's Disease, which in those days was called St. Vitus's Dance, and he lived his entire life there in the family home. Until he was old, he had kept a large garden and enough poultry in the barn to carry on a business of selling produce and eggs, and children up in that neighborhood of Lincoln Street and Ford Street and Slayton Terrace referred to him fondly as "the egg man." He had twinkling, astonishingly bright blue eyes and a ready smile and a friendly manner. But, as both Al and Inez each in their own way told me in some confidence, the arrangement of three there in the house was not an ideal one. Al evidently did his best to be pleasant to Elmer but maintained that Elmer did not respond in kind and didn't care for him. Part of the problem may have been Al's flatland inability to understand the natural Yankee taciturnity and to accept some measure of it in their day-to-day lives. To Elmer, Al would have, and evidently did, seem noisy and verbose. But for whatever reason, much of the time three was a crowd in Inez's household, and when she found herself in the middle of a situation, as she used to admit to me, she would show a partiality to her brother: "Blood's thicker than water," she would say. Winters were most difficult, when she was working and it was difficult for Al to be out and about. At least they had their evenings to themselves, as Elmer kept a farmer's hours all his life, rising with the sun and, after an early supper, retiring to his room behind the kitchen for the night. And for a number of years during Inez's time off in the summer, she and Al managed a week or so in Maine, where they would rent a cottage at Ogunquit and Al would indulge his great love of seafood. On postcards he'd send me from there, he would report on some of the delicious meals he had enjoyed; lobsters were so much his favorite that he once told me that he was thinking of having a lobster carved on his gravestone with the epitaph "Here's a guy who really loved 'em."

I first began getting to know Al when he was working as night desk clerk at the White Cupboard Inn on the square in the center of Woodstock. The lobby and reception area of that old hotel were right next to the new bar on the west side of the building, which, for a few years, was a favorite hang-out for a number of us young people. By the time Al came to work at 10:30 or 11:00, spirits were high, and when he looked in at our group, he was always cheerfully received. Having tried out a couple of jokes on us one evening and found they went over well (one about a group of rubes from Quechee, Vermont who got separated in Boston nearly laid out an old friend of mine before he recovered), Al began regularly appearing with other jokes that he had collected and kept filed away on 3 by 5 cards. He'd wander in from the lobby to a rousing welcome, clean shaven with his hair slicked back and nattily attired in gray flannel slacks, wing-tip shoes, pinstriped shirt and club or rep tie, plaid vest with a watch chain, and Harris tweed sports jacket, and after some conversation about his golf game or the current fortunes of the Red Sox, we'd ask him if he had any good ones for us. He would then, without a word, fix us with a serious and intent gaze as he fumbled around in the inside pocket of his jacket, and out would come the typed cards, which had the lead-in on one side and the punch line on the other. Some of these, it seemed, he had not looked at in years, and he would simply read them off as he came to them, occasionally becoming confused by his own typos; and sometimes the punch line on the back would have been inaccurately transcribed or recalled between the time of hearing the joke— perhaps from a traveling salesman or at a Shriners' convention years before—and the time of typing it out, so that it made little or no sense and left him puzzled and looking at us quizzically for some help in "getting it" or at least in understanding what it meant. And at that point we would always be nearly on the floor with laughter. For, in many cases, the mistakes and the whole confused performance, when it occurred, would be better than the jokes, some of which were pretty dated.

Al and Inez loved company and were always pleased to see me, though Inez liked it best when Maria and I both stopped to visit them during our times at home with my parents during school vacations. On summer evenings we usually made our visits at that time when they would most likely have just finished their supper at the picnic table in the yard and would be enjoying the early evening air and Al would be pacing about with a cigar. Before we could sit down, Inez would walk us around to show us the cultivated and wild flowers that were then in bloom. She was especially fond of all the lupin in the field to the east of their house. Al would hasten inside to the fridge to get me a beer, and we would catch up by letting each other know what'd we'd been up to. He'd ask me about my work and my travels, and he'd tell me about his night desk clerk jobs at the Inn or the Shiretown Motel or wherever he was working at the time, or about his sales and what plans he had to expand his line and increase his territory; and a second beer would usually include a half-serious toast to "the big time," where it seemed to him we were both headed. Then sometimes, especially during our winter visits, Inez would bring out some old photo albums to show us. Once Maria and I agreed to take them on in Scrabble, which turned out to be embarrassing for us all. The game was preceded by their speculating on what little chance they'd have against a couple of teachers with college degrees, so it was unsettling when they beat us badly—Maria had never played the game before, and I had played only a couple of times when I was in high school, and Al and Inez were seasoned pros. It was no contest, and, to our relief, we were never invited to play them again.

Al and I had certain things we tried to do together every year. He was especially fond of a restaurant in West Bridge-water called The Pancake House, and we made sure to go there at least once a year for a big brunch of pancakes or waffles and home fries and sausage. And, from the time I introduced him to it, we had a standing arrangement to go together to the St. James Episcopal Church Fair, which was held on the second Thursday in July. I was interested in the fair primarily because of the book tent with it large assortment of used books, and the clothes bazaar, where I would look for neckties and good used sport coats. Since it was first-come, first-serve, it was important to arrive at the church early to browse and then line up and wait for the church bell to strike 10 o'clock and the fair to open. Al was always raring to go. Usually on the night before, I would receive a couple of phone calls from him, checking on the time when I'd be picking him up on the following morning, and the next day my mother, on her way up the hill from running an errand in town, would report seeing him standing at the bottom of his driveway working on his first cigar of the day as early as 8:45 in anticipation of our arranged meeting time of 9:30. Every year we recalled our previous discoveries at the fair and laughed over a couple of mishaps. The first time we went to it together, we were at the head of the line for the clothes bazaar, which was always located on the lawn at the north side of the church, and Al snagged a very nice, barely worn tweed sport coat and a couple of almost new club ties, "real corkers," as he liked to say. When he went to pay for them, the regular cashier, Barbara Hall, was not at her usual place, and her replacement, Richard Marble, was just getting set up at his table. Mr. Marble, a distinguished older gentleman, was a Harvardian who had served for a time as principal of Woodstock High School, and he was the village's recognized ornithologist. This was his first time on the job of cashier, and Al was his first customer. As Al reached for his wallet, Mr. Marble told him the price of his purchases, which for some reason turned out to be even less than he had antici-pated, and in his excitement his stomach played him false, and he stepped behind a nearby, small elm tree and lost his breakfast. For years afterwards, we wondered whether Mr. Marble, at that moment, had had serious second thoughts about what he had let himself in for in his new job. All of the items on sale at the fair—food, books and records, clothes, household utensils, furniture, kitchenware, sports equipment, woodland plants—were donated by people throughout the year and sorted and neatly arranged on display under the tents and outside them on the church green and side lawns. One year, Al spotted a very nice seersucker suit and purchased it for the usual small price. He also bought at the food tent a carton of homemade baked beans to take home for supper. As I had left the fair early, he had to walk home, and as he was doing so, without realizing it, he managed to tilt the beans so that some of the sauce ran out of the carton and onto the suit, which he was carrying over his arm. Later that afternoon when he went to show Inez the suit, they realized what had happened, and to make matters worse, she recognized the suit as one of Al's own that she had donated to the fair the year before because it no longer fit him. He had bought back his own outcast suit and soiled it so that they had a dry cleaning charge to pay before Inez could donate it to next year's fair.

Although our get-togethers usually occurred at 25 Lincoln Street, in the summer of 1967, Al and Inez came to two parties at our house—one to celebrate my sister Jane's high school graduation, and one in August for my father's 60th birthday. Both of them were small gatherings for family and a few close friends, including "Aunt" Ada Maynes. I remember being out on the porch sweeping the steps and straightening the wicker furniture in preparation for Jane's party, when I heard some conversation from down the street and went to the bottom of the driveway to see Al and Inez approaching. She was carrying a bouquet of flowers, and Al was some 15 yards ahead of her in his excitement, dressed up in light summer slacks and sport coat and puffing a cigar. For years afterward, he liked to recall that party as the only time in his life he had ever held a glass of champagne in one hand and, at the same time, a gin and tonic in the other. At times like this, when life was good, he would shout out the old Jackie Gleason line from "The Honeymooners," "How sweet it is!" At the height of the evening, he asked me if he could speak with me in private for just a moment out in the front hall. He wondered if I thought it would be appropriate for him to give us a couple of songs in honor of the occasion. Al had a more than passable tenor voice, and he very much enjoyed singing. For a number of years he was an associate member of the Mount Sinai Temple in Montpelier, where he sang with the Chanters. He favored the music of the old barbershop quartets and of the crooners of the 20s, and he liked the vocalists of the big band era. I told him we'd be pleased to hear him and that I would act as his stage manager. So I stepped back into the living room and announced that Al was going to provide a little something special for the evening, and when he was ready to go on, I'd blink the lights in the front hall as a signal for their attention. Al took a quick look in the hall mirror, thought for a moment, announced that he was ready, and then made his entry. He sang "The Rocky Road to Dublin" and "When Irish Eyes Are Smiling" in special consideration of Aunt Ada, who was Irish, and then he finished with a good imitation of Eddie Cantor's comic version of "Margie," which ends with "We'll wine and dine the whole night through. And when we have had our fill, do you know who'll pay the bill? Oh, Margie, Margie, it's you." The entertainment came not only from the songs, which were pretty well delivered, but also from the way he took us back to an earlier time, a time to which, all of his life, he really belonged. It was as though in that performance we were watching and hearing Al Powers' being most fully and completely himself. He had no capacity for any sort of affectation, and there was nothing of the showoff about him, but instead sincerity and a great and winning will to please. There was, as I understand more clearly now than ever, no one remotely like him.

Of our times in the summer, two moments in particular are most clearly imprinted on my memory, in part because both Al and Inez spoke of them for years afterward. In 1966, I decided to spend my summer vacation with my friend Bob Anderson and his family in Easton, Maryland on the eastern shore of the Chesapeake if I could find a job down there. The hope was that I could work for a friend of the Andersons who was a documentary filmmaker. But after a couple of weeks of crab fishing on the Miles River and suffering sunstroke and nearly being devoured by the largest mosquitoes I have ever seen while I waited for the film maker to make up his mind, I decided in late June to pack it in and head north, where at least the nights were cool. So I spent two days bussing it back to Vermont, arriving in Woodstock in the early evening. Having said nothing to my parents or anyone else about my change of plans, I decided to walk home with my suitcase from the square, where the Greyhound had let me off. I had returned before the tourist inundation, and Central Street was quiet. Woodstock had never seemed more welcoming, and I wondered why I had even considered being elsewhere that summer. On my way up the hill in the early summer evening light, it occurred to me to surprise Al and Inez and then phone my parents from there. So I walked up around their driveway and found them still sitting, just as I hoped they would be, at the picnic table after their supper, and I don't think I have ever received a more heartfelt welcome from anyone. Al had been very disappointed to hear that I would most likely be away for the summer, and suddenly here I was, home until September, in time for the Episcopal Church Fair and with more than two months stretching before us. He was instantly into the house and out carrying a couple of "cold ones" as he called the bottles of Bud he kept on hand, and Inez, explaining that I was not too late, led me across the yard to show me her lupin, still blooming in the uncut grass. The other indelible moment comes from the summer of 1968. Inez invited my mother and father and me down to their house for lunch on the 4th of July to celebrate the holiday with the traditional New England meal of salmon, new potatoes, and peas, with apple pie and ice cream for dessert. Unfortunately, my father could not join us because he had to work that day at the holiday festivities being held in Bailey's Meadow, one of the main attractions of which were a group of skydivers who were scheduled to make a number of jumps at specified times throughout the afternoon, landing in the fields by the Ottauquechee River. Mother and I walked down to their house about noon and joined Al and Inez there at the picnic table with its bouquet and tablecloth. The meal was delicious, and when the time came, we went to the front lawn to take advantage of its grand view over the valley and watch for the skydivers. When the plane came over, we had the perfect spot to see the tiny figures at what seemed a tremendous height, spill out of the plane and fall until they pulled the rip cords to fill their chutes with air and drift slowly down where the treetops obscured their coming to rest on the ground. It was one of those perfect days that, even as they are happening, have a way of showing themselves as though from a long way off, insuring us that they will remain in the memory in all their particulars for a very long time to come.

As Al and Inez advanced in years, the Vermont winters seemed longer to them and, especially to Al, more confining. As he was always, in a way, odd man out in that house, he came to feel isolated, especially on days when the cold weather or the ice and snow prevented him from getting out and about to peddle his wares, and, Inez being at work, he was stuck with Elmer, who tended to rebuff his well meaning attempts at conversation. Finally, one winter he'd had enough of it and told me he had applied for and landed a hotel job as desk clerk, with room and board, somewhere, as I recall, in the Poconos. I was astonished at the news, though I soon came to realize I shouldn't have been. As he explained it, it wasn't just the situation at home and the prospect of another long winter of being cooped up there that prompted him to hit the road, but also the fact that there was "nothing moving" in Woodstock and the neighboring towns at that time of year. Though he was in his early 70s at that time, he was still looking ahead, still driven by the energy of his younger days in the Roaring Twenties and fueled by post World War II optimism, and he still had a kind of Jimmy Durante pluck about him. If he was down about something, he wasn't going to stay down for long. He told me of his plans during the 1968 Thanksgiving holidays, and sometime not long afterward, he sent me the projected date of his departure from Woodstock and his itinerary: he'd be catching a bus to New York and changing there for his destination in Pennsylvania, and by the looks of the schedule, he'd have a bit of a layover in the evening at Port Authority. Since mid-town Manhattan was a seedy and tough place in those days before the cleanup under Mayor Giuliani, and I was worried that he might miss his connection and have to hang around there for a while at night, I told him I'd hop a bus from Rutherford, New Jersey, where I was living then, and meet him there for a bite to eat and a drink and pass the time with him. Though I arrived early on the designated evening and waited through his scheduled arrival time, he didn't appear. When I inquired of some of the attendants if they had noticed someone of Al's description getting off a Vermont bus, one of them remembered him well, as he had assisted him in getting to his next bus shortly after his arrival. Evidently, we had somehow gotten our signals crossed, and though I had looked forward to seeing him, it was a relief to know he was safely on his way. And I guess it was a reminder to me that he was not, after all, some hayseed from up country easily disoriented by the big city, but a cosmopolitan at heart and still perfectly capable of taking care of himself in most urban situations. When I was next in Woodstock that winter, I stopped in to see Inez and find out what she had heard from him. Though she let me know once again that she had been very much against his decision to go away for the winter, she reported that he had been writing to her regularly. He and I corresponded some throughout his time away, mostly through postcards and brief notes, and it was some months later that I learned of his intention to return home in April. In fact, as it turned out, I was back in Woodstock for my spring break from school at the time when he was scheduled to arrive, and Inez asked me of I could drive her car over to Rutland to pick him up at the bus station in the evening. It was a cold April and well after dark by the time his bus came in, and I was there to meet him when he stepped off it. I was shocked at his appearance: he was thin and gaunt and pale and had a hacking cough. As he explained, he had caught the flu sometime in the late winter and was having trouble recovering from it fully. We retrieved his suitcase and then set out for Woodstock. On the way we talked about his time away, and I gathered that, while his job and his living conditions had been suitable, they had not, perhaps, met his highest hopes, and he had not been well satisfied with the food. I was worried about his health—though he didn't seem to be—and also sorry that he hadn't been able to make a better recovery before returning home because I thought his condition would give Inez and Elmer the advantage in maintaining that he'd been a fool to leave home and go away in the first place. And I couldn't help wondering what sort of homecoming he would receive when we arrived. I can well remember that as we pulled up around the driveway, the outside light was on for us. When we walked through the kitchen door—he with his briefcase and some small gifts he had brought, and I with his suitcase— he said, "Hi, honey" and gave her a peck on the cheek. When he stepped back, she was as shocked by his appearance as I had been. During the short time I stayed there, they seemed to have little to say, so I refused Inez's offer to pay me for my chauffeur services and bid them goodnight so that they could catch up or become reacquainted or whatever was to happen between them after their separation of five months or so. Al gradually regained his health as the weather became warmer, and things went back pretty much to the way they had been before he went away.

In all the years that I knew Al, he was always active in one way or another. He stayed busy when the weather was such that he could be out and about, and he let me know in his letters how his sales were going:

Bruce, I'm really beginning to click with my book matches and also with my Brite View Cleaners. I just ordered four dozen more of them and I plan on ordering twelve dozen more the first of June. As I've found from past experience, the market is wide open. I really feel that I hit the jackpot last week as a man from Burlington gave me an order of book matches but the real thrill I received was on last Tuesday as I wrote up an order for 40,000—16 cases— from my friend Raymond P. Buskey, the owner of the Inn Garage in Hanover N.H.

Such were his successes, and they were evidently what kept him going. We corresponded when I was again away in London on a sabbatical in 1976-77, and visited them whenever we came back to Woodstock throughout the rest of that decade. What I don't remember for certain is my last time with Inez, but Maria clearly recalls last seeing her in the middle of the summer of 1980. She was driving through town on an errand, and she spotted Maria and pulled over for a brief chat. Though she confessed to being depressed, otherwise, she seemed to be in good health. Thus, it came as a great shock to us when we heard not long afterwards that she had died on July 25th in Dartmouth-Hitchcock Hospital, where she had gone to be treated, I think, for a heart condition. Unfortunately, a court date prevented my making the trip from Connecticut to Woodstock to attend her funeral.

My friendship with Inez was rooted in the past. She would tell people, "Bruce and I both love the old days." We especially loved the village of Woodstock as it had been, and we never tired of recalling people long since gone and places that had disappeared or had been altered beyond recognition, like her uncle Earl Slack's store on Central Street, which had closed in 1963. She had known the Coffin family all her life. As a neighbor, she had been well acquainted with my grandparents, and she was a classmate and friend of my father's oldest brother James Hazen. When she and I began reminiscing, Al would listen and every once in a while contribute something as he heard the name of someone he had known, but he did not belong to Woodstock as Inez did, and his mind was not tuned to its history in the way hers was.

At the time of Inez's sudden death, I was worried about Al and wondered what he would do without her. I couldn't imagine him staying on at their house with Elmer and relying on someone with a car to provide them with groceries and take them to their appointments. For a while, Inez's friend Catherine Fish and her husband Gordon helped them out, but for Al, being dependent in that way and being there without Inez was, finally, intolerable. I assumed that when he did leave, it would be for the Homestead, Woodstock's home for senior citizens. After all, living there would enable him to walk into the center of the village and back to peddle his products, and he could still find rides to and from the other towns to fill the orders of his other customers. Therefore I was stunned when he told me that he had decided to leave Woodstock entirely for the Elks Home in Bedford, Virginia. I hoped he would change his mind, but in early November, a little over three months after Inez's death, I received a letter from him written on National Home of the Benevolent Protectorate Order of Elks stationery, saying that an old friend had driven him down there in late October for a short trial period and that the place was satisfying his expectations: he was meeting friendly people, the food was good and there was "plenty of it," and he was within easy access of the center of Bedford, which was "just a mile from the Home, only a buck to go down there in a taxi." And he announced that "after giving the matter full consideration, it looks as though it is the right course to follow." His plan was to return to Woodstock long enough to complete the necessary application procedures—which included a physical exam and the gathering of references from the Hartford Lodge—and then to have Fred Doubleday, a friend, drive him to Bedford to his new home. He returned to Woodstock in mid-November and remained there for the better part of the winter before making the move. During this time, the Fishes looked out for him, and Al was happy to report that he had treated Gordon to an all-you-can-eat dinner at the Owl's Nest in Lebanon, New Hampshire and had amazed him by "put[ting] away 18 oysters on the half shell, six pieces of shrimp, three plates of Alaska crab, topped off with strawberries and vanilla ice cream," thus demonstrating that his appetite for seafood had suffered no decline. Nor had his social impulses: he arranged to have Catherine "do a job with refreshments" for a few of his friends on his 83rd birthday on Christmas Eve at his house. Since Maria and I and the children were having our Christmas at home in Connecticut, the best I could was to phone him that night as the party was in full swing. He was pleased to receive my call and said that, though he missed Inez terribly, he was having a good time with friends and was managing to make the best of things. Two months or so later he left for Virginia, as planned, and, we continued to exchange letters and cards for a time, as did he and my parents. He died there on March 11, 1986.

For some years after Al had moved away, Elmer stayed on at the house alone, again Catherine and Gordon Fish and others doing his food shopping for him and helping him out, until he finally went to spend his last years at the Hanover Terrace Nursing Home, where he lived until his death at age 87 in the spring of 1990. During the better part of the decade in which first Inez and then Al and then Elmer disappeared, their house and land at 25 Lincoln Street looked—strangely, to us who had known them—very much the same. When I told my parents that every time I passed it I simply could not believe that those people were not still there at home, they said they felt the same way, especially in June when, even in their absence, we would see Inez's lupin standing forth in the field grass under the early summer sun, nodding in the wind, as though for her approval. Eventually, however, the property, which had been left to her daughter, fell victim to the real estate market and was sold to some people from Montana who specialized in flipping houses. They lived there while they were doing most of the renovation work themselves, gutting the inside, turning the attic into a third-floor living space, and putting a wide porch around three sides, then sold it. Either they or some subsequent owner not long afterward divided the property, and a large modern house and steep driveway were built on the sloping eastern end of the field occupied by the lupin. Sic transit gloria mundi.

I have continued to be troubled by the question of whether Al made the right choice in electing to spend his last years away from Woodstock. In the last of the letters we exchanged, he mentioned receiving visits from his daughter and son-in-law, who lived in St Albans, West Virginia, so that his being in Virginia at least enabled them to spend more time together than they ever had and to get to know each other better. The only person from Woodstock, to my knowledge, to see Al at the Elks Home was Dick Tracy, Sr., a golfing friend of his, and I recall his telling me that Al was, of course, making the best of things, but that he seemed somewhat lonely. And that is the way I feared he ultimately would be, and the way I see him in the last and, regrettably, the only photograph I have of him, which he sent me late in life after he had joined the choir of St. Johns Episcopal Church in Bedford. It is a color photo of him standing by himself outside the church on a sunny day in his vestments—bright red choir robe and white surplice. He is smiling as always, though he looks older and thinner, and his face is pale. And I cannot look at it without wondering whether, in the final reckoning, he regretted not living out his final years in Woodstock among so many people who knew him.

In the years since his death, I have also wondered about our friendship, which was deeper but also harder for me to understand than my friendship with his wife. He was always more curious about the details of my life than she was. When I was boning up on Spanish in order to satisfy the foreign language requirement for my MA in English from New York University, Al went so far as to purchase a Spanish-English dictionary so that we could exchange a few words in another language when we got together, and he used to have me quiz him; for some reason—perhaps a recollection of his days at law school—"abogado," the Spanish word for lawyer, was the first one he learned, and he delighted in assuring me that he had plenty of "cerveza" on hand for my forthcoming visits. And he'd ask me to critique his pronunciation, which quite often needed correction: for example, he had for many years known and corresponded with someone in La Jolla, California and was astonished to hear that it was pronounced "La Hoya" and not as it was spelled. He had a surprising number of friends around the country, and he always looked out and away. It was typical of him to mention, right away, in his letter from his trial period in the Elks Home, that he had "had the good fortune of meeting several of the different brothers, from many of the states, some as far away as New Mexico." I have come to think that, unlike Inez, what he valued in me was not so much my belonging to Woodstock as my having at least partially separated myself from it, for the years when I knew him were the most rootless and adventurous of my life, and Al always wanted to know all about places where I had lived or traveled to. In our conversations and in my letters to him, he was, I suppose, sharing vicariously my life at that time, which he was convinced would have suited him just fine.

One of the distinguishing features in our relationships with the people who mean most to us is our need to imagine and reimagine their lives as they were before we knew them, and it is as natural for us to do this as it is for us to feel their presence after they are gone. In the late summer of 1993 when Maria and I and Jonathan drove Lizzie out to Grinnell College in Iowa, we happened to pass through the town of Newton, and somewhere just within the town limits, I realized that this was the home of The Newton Manufacturing Company, whose products Al had drummed for so many years. Then suddenly, there was the sign and, behind it, the large production buildings of the company, right next to us on the left side of the street. I was astonished. Here was a place Al had never seen but had corresponded with and received his orders from for years, a place which, had he entered its doors, would, I like to think, have greeted him as one of their own. Would they, I wondered, still have, somewhere among their records, his name and some compilation of his sales over so many years? We drove on by, and my strange excitement was tinged by dismay that it was years too late to tell Al about this odd coincidence, which brought him suddenly very much into the moment at the same time that it placed him at an irrecoverable distance. What I did not realize then that I have since come to consider is that the experience of that moment—its peculiar intensity—came from a half realized sense that I was living something for him, and my excitement and wonder were as great as they were because they were his as well as my own. Newton, Iowa was his place more than it was mine, just as our friendship, though it took place in Woodstock, Vermont, was, in many ways, all about places beyond it.

My mother perfectly explained Al Powers, as she often had a way of doing with people, in a word. It was at the time when he had finally made up his mind to go to Virginia and I was trying to understand why he'd leave a place that had been home to him for over thirty years of married life, not to speak of his childhood times with his grandparents. She too had evidently been pondering the same question, and she said, "Well, you know, Bruce, he's a drifter—don't you think?" I was struck dumb by the accuracy of the word. That is exactly what he was. It is what prompted him to take his various hotel jobs, to go off to the Poconos all by himself in the winter at an advanced age, and to finish his life in Virginia. And it was what made him always curious about where I'd been, and ready to strike out for new territory where there were people he hadn't met and places he hadn't seen, new prospects, chances to discover a new line, maybe, and to knock 'em dead. Unlike so many of the people in my family and so many of the people I had known in my life in Vermont who were contented with staying in the place where they were born and felt no need to travel, Al was, his life in Woodstock notwithstanding, a man of no fixed address. In his character and his outlook he had something of Arthur Miller's salesman, Willy Loman, about him, as he is described by his friend Charlie in the "Requiem" in *Death of a Salesman*: "There's no rock bottom to the life. . . . He's a man way out there in the blue, riding on a smile and a shoeshine. . . . A salesman is got to dream, boy. It comes with the territory." And he certainly would have understood the speaker in the Larkin poem who says, "No, I have never found/The place where I could say/This is my proper ground,/Here I shall stay." He was a throwback to another era—a product of Dale Carnegie and Horatio Alger, a believer in the American dream, who never gave up the hope that success was just around the corner, and it made sense that I should rediscover him so fully in a moment, out there on the road, as I was passing through Iowa, so far away from the place in which I knew him.

Al is fixed forever in my memory by the last thing he ever said to me when I visited him shortly before he went away. I was home for a weekend in the winter of 1980-81, partly to visit my parents and partly to see Al just before he left Woodstock. I stopped by his house in the evening; the outside light was on as it always had been when guests were expected. Though I had been in the house once or twice since Inez died, it still seemed strange not to see her and be greeted by her in the kitchen. Elmer had retired for the night. We had a drink in the living room and then went upstairs to the place Al called his "den." It was a small room with a desk and a cot. On the floor was the green rug that Inez had bought for him years before, and on the walls were group photos of Shriners taken at charity events, framed certificates of achievement in sales, a Red Sox team photo, some cards with inspirational verses, and an extraordinary photo of Al in his heyday, hair slicked back, big, "how sweet it is" smile on his face, just coming around on a golf swing. Some of these things he'd be taking with him, many of them he'd be leaving behind. One suitcase was half packed, and he had closed up his portable typewriter, on which he always typed his letters. He opened his closet and showed me his tie rack and told me to pick out any that I liked, and I found two or three. The second floor of the house with its fully furnished but mostly unused bedrooms seemed huge and lonely. Back downstairs, we had a nightcap in the living room; neither of us was in any hurry to say goodbye, and all the while I was wondering what it must be like for him to be about to leave Woodstock. I thought about all the people he had known and still knew here and, for some reason, all the nights he had passed in the village in his job as night clerk and how long some of them must have seemed. I imagined him chatting up the Woodstock Inn's night watchman to help pass the time, and I wondered if the great lamp-lit lobby of that historic building, with its couches and stuffed chairs, might have brought back memories of all the hotels he had worked in. In his nights at the White Cupboard Inn, would the policeman on duty just outside have visited him on his nightly rounds or relieved some of the boredom of sitting in his car by stopping in to talk with him? How many times had Al gotten up from his place at the front desk there to look out the windows, and did the silent and deserted square under its dim streetlights awaken in him an affection for this village where he had come to spend so many years of his life, or did it seem just a momentary still life in a long whistle stop on a journey meant to take him out and away? At least on this night, it was hard to believe that he was not looking back as much as he was looking ahead. When it came time for me to leave, we put on our coats and stepped outside. Snow was piled on both sides of the driveway, but it was a fairly mild night for late winter, and a big moon shone over the barn, illuminating its roof and passing in and out of swiftly moving clouds. I made some remark to the effect that he had spent a good many years at this place. And, as we stood looking over at the mostly darkened house, he replied with an anecdote which, for me, expresses something of the personality of Al Powers and captures the times he belonged to and the spirit of his life more fully than any words I ever heard him utter: "You know," he said, "it's like that story of Calvin Coolidge, Silent Cal, when he was president. Some people spotted him and Mrs. Coolidge out in Washington for a short evening stroll (different times then, they probably wouldn't have had many security people with them), and pretending they didn't recognize the president and first lady, they pointed to the White House and said, 'Excuse me, sir, but could you tell us who lives there?' To which Coolidge replied, 'Nobody, they just come and go.'"

I shook hands with him then, wished him all the best, and I walked slowly the short distance home. I never saw him again.

Recovery

For a time after I finished college and moved first to New Jersey and then to England, I was cut off from my extended family in Vermont. A dutiful correspondent, I kept up with my parents by letter and postcards, but I lost touch with my aunts and uncles. That is not to say that I forgot about them, for I could have called back their place in my childhood experiences if I had been asked to do so. But they belonged to the past, which was a well-furnished room left to itself behind a closed door, sealed up for the sake of the time at hand and the huge future opening out of it with its infinite possibilities carrying me so far away that my early life seemed a long time ago. For the two years in my late twenties when I was living and working in London, I came to love that great city so much that I intended to settle there as an expatriate and to spend a month or so with my mother and father in Woodstock every summer. About the rest of the family, whatever information my parents thought to pass on to me would be enough. During one of my brief times at home, my mother told me that my Aunt Julia and Uncle Gale might like to see me, and she wondered whether I'd be interested in going with her to pay them a visit in nearby Plymouth, where they lived. I had not seen them for years, and I agreed to go along primarily out of a sense of family obligation and a wish to please my mother.

Of my mother's three sisters, Julia was the closest to her in age and the favorite aunt of my twin brother, my sister and myself. With her dark hair and brown eyes, she was also the prettiest and the liveliest, and her somewhat husky voice crackled with good humor and affection. Her love of fun and her interest in us, her nephews, always had us looking for her right away at family gatherings and wading through everyone else to get to her. To her siblings and to her parents, however, she was, as she later told me, a source of worry because of her choice of a husband. All of his life, Gale was something of a roustabout. He was generous to a fault, drank too much, drove too fast, loved animals and children, was a wonderful dancer, liked to raise hell, and had been married and divorced by the time Julia met him and found him irresistible. Their one son, Abe, was three years younger than my brother and I and one of our main childhood companions.

Probably because my mother knew me better than I knew myself in some ways, on the bright and cool late summer morning when we set out to visit Julia and Gale, rather than asking me to drive as she often did, she herself got behind the wheel of the car. For the first part of our short journey along Route 4 west, where the Ottauquechee River passes through a familiar pastoral landscape, we made idle conversation about events that had occurred during my year away and about old friends I had not yet taken the time to see since I had arrived home. Then, some four miles out of Woodstock, where the valley narrows and the remains of what were once fields and pastures of small farms give way to woods along steeply rising hills, the town of Bridgewater announced itself by its road sign and its situation, and commanded our attention. As one of those New England valley towns strung out along the road that passes through it, Bridgewater has no streets as such and no sidewalks, and shows little evidence of commercial activity. It appears to display to the traveler all that it is and is not in one viewing. In its heyday in the first half of the twentieth century, what kept it going was its woolen mill, which gave employment to its working class population, including, at times, Aunt Julia and Uncle Gale. And it was here that Uncle Gale was born, the middle child of twelve surviving children. As was often the case in those days, the mill claimed him from an early age; when little more than a child, he was employed as a sort of go-between to carry bootleg liquor from the suppliers to the mill workers between their shifts, and he quit school early to go to work there himself. From the busy town of those early years, the Bridgewater that my mother and I were driving through that day was becoming the largely depressed village of today. Its mill had recently shut down, and mostly what we were seeing were the vestiges of going concerns: Robinson's Store was an empty building; the stylish stucco and timber, mock Tudor building that had housed both the village post office and the mill's fashionable store for its fine woolen goods was closed; the gas station was on the way out. Down by the river behind the mill, the large tenement building where at least one of Gale's sisters and her family had lived was gone, and in its place was an empty lot. West of there and still poised precariously on the bank high above the river as it always had been was the store that had for years been owned and operated by Bump Davis, an ageless man who sold groceries and beer and various household items and usually managed to let his customers know before they left that he was a certified major league baseball scout. Even when it was a going concern, the place looked as though it had been boarded up and closed for years, and we noticed that its new proprietor had let it sink further into decrepitude, as he had done with the large tenement across the street. In the middle of town in a flat-roofed, two-story building obviously built for commercial purposes was the Bridgewater Tavern, the town's only bar and restaurant, which had managed to hang on through a number of owners; and, as we slowly drove by, it began to return me to the times of my childhood spent there with my aunt and uncle.

Back then in the 1940s and 50s, the Bridgewater Tavern had been known locally as Solger's Bar and Restaurant. It was a rollicking place where mill workers could cash their checks and spend their wages, and it was there that we were usually taken on Saturday nights when we had gone up to stay the weekend with Julia and Gale and Abe. The five of us would crowd into a booth in the noisy, sweaty, smoke-filled bar room to join the crowd in celebrating payday and the end of another week. The three of us youngsters were treated to hot dogs, hamburgers, cokes, French fries, anything we wanted, including an endless supply of nickels and dimes to feed the juke box, which never stopped playing and which seemed to get louder to compete with the rising volume of the growing crowd. Howard and I had never seen so much money, let alone watched it change hands in such a short time. Whole families would be packed in there, and many of the people were relatives in some way of Gale's. The men in their work clothes were big and beer-bellied and swaggering, the women tough and watchful, their children lively, but a little wary at first of my brother and me, who were relative strangers. The language was coarse, the conversation included a great deal of exaggeration, challenge, and rough good humor. The mood was warm and expansive, and as children we were patted and tousled and pinched and hugged and invited to flex our muscles and made much of in general. By the time various stages of drunkenness and amorousness were reached and things turned volatile and sometimes down-right ugly, as they had a tendency to do, we would have left with a crowd of revelers bound for Julia and Gale's house to watch Saturday night wrestling on their television set.

Their house was one of four small dwellings situated on an acre or so of land on the side of a hill on a back road at the west end of the village. Two of these houses belonged to Gale's brothers. One of the three houses was well kept and nicely landscaped; the other two, including Julia and Gale's, looked inside and out as though the carpenters had for some reason walked off the job. One wall of the downstairs bedroom had never been finished with wallboard or plaster so that it stood there with exposed joists. Next to the bedroom, the house's one bathroom had plumbing which worked only some of the time and often required buckets of water to flush the toilet. Upstairs was one long unfinished room under the eaves. But on Saturday nights at wrestling time the place could have been Madison Square Garden itself. Crammed into the small living room, people sat on chairs, on the arms of chairs, on laps, on the floor, or simply stood in what space remained. The drinking resumed, if in fact it had ever stopped, the cigarette smoke made even less visible the action on the small black and white TV screen, whose reception was at best clouded and snowy. No matter, this was one of the few television sets in Bridgewater at that time, and as the matches went on, the excitement and hilarity increased: the crowd shouted their encouragement to their favorites, including advice about what body parts to seize and hold onto and mutilate, excoriated anything that might be construed as cowardice, let alone caution, argued with the advertisements, swore at the TV set when the picture faded or went momentarily haywire, cursed the referees and even the announcer, Jack Brickhouse, whom they insisted on calling "Brick Shithouse." Sometime before the broadcast went off the air, my brother and I and Abe climbed the stairs and went to bed, usually discovering that we were tired enough to forego the comic books and drop off to sleep in spite of the roaring from the living room. Recalling those times now as we reached the west end of the village and noticed the road that led up to where my aunt and uncle had lived, I reminded my mother that even though I was, as a child, so dreadfully susceptible to homesickness that I didn't join my brother when he went to stay over night with relatives, I always felt myself enough at home with Julia and Gale to be able to face and get through the night away from my mother and father.

Bridgewater, I was being reminded on this morning as we passed through it, is always Bridgewater, a memorable place in its way, gritty, unpretentious, struggling and surviving with its soul intact. That is not to say that back then in its tough working class world of mill and tavern there were no casualties. Some of the poverty that showed itself then was still in evidence, and even Mother and I, with our largely hearsay knowledge of people there, could bring to mind some young lives darkened by disadvantaged circumstances and some failed marriages and broken families resulting from alcoholism and philandering. Fights occurred in Solger's Bar, and Monday mornings would sometimes find workmen taking down makeshift plywood and putting new plate glass in one or both of the big front windows. Remembering some of the waitresses who worked there, I thought of one well kept, rather harmless looking man who had been a notorious womanizer and home wrecker in his day, and I recalled his long obituary, which consisted mainly of the names of children he had sired with various wives and partners. And, catching sight of the Ottauquechee River running under its heavily wooded ridges along the west end of town, I remembered a woman who had left Bridgewater after a failed marriage only to return years later as a middle-aged alcoholic estranged from her children, and take her own life down along the river upstream from the mill, killing herself slowly with multiple shots from a .22 caliber rifle. Bridgewater had had its dark chapters, its losses, but those had in some way deepened its character and made it a more intensely human place. And I wondered at the curious way in which the name of the village itself so often brought before the mind's eye an ambiguous and enduring image from times when I had seen it in November at the end of another hunting season. Under lowering skies with afternoon starting to shut down and the hills with their leafless trees seeming to frown on the backs of the buildings in the valley as they awaited the first snow, a gutted deer hangs from a pulley next to an old pickup in a front yard full of trampled grass and faded flowers. But the windows of all the houses are lamp-lit against the oncoming, long night, and wood smoke is rising from the chimneys, and something in me which must have originated with those times at my aunt and uncle's surprises me, Woodstock boy that I am, by whispering, "my people" and "home."

As we left the center of the village where Bridgewater peters out into a string of houses along the river, we came to Bridgewater Corners, and before we turned onto Route 100A to Plymouth, I caught sight of the road that leads to Bridgewater Center and beyond that into the huge tract of wilderness known as Bridgewater Chateauguay. Perhaps Gale would have spent more time fixing up his house if he had not been so drawn to the outdoors, where he enjoyed hunting, fishing, walking with his rabbit dogs, and exploring the land in general. Our times with him and Julia were always in one way or another adventures which we could describe excitedly to our parents when we returned home. Though Howard and I, as children, had some fear of water, with Gale's gentle encouragement and resourcefulness both of us overcame that fear and learned to swim under water at The Branch, a place where the cold brook from Chateauguay emerged from deep woods into a small clearing and formed a kind of pool just beyond one of the many bridges that crossed it. He would teach us to stand on his submerged shoulders and push off from them at various heights and to step into his hand to be tossed into the air for a cannonball, and, like a colossus, he would stand in the deep parts and challenge us to swim between his legs and bring up the white stones he had tossed in the water for us to retrieve. And Julia would be there, splashing around with us or getting the picnic lunch ready. Sometimes Gale's sister Evelyn and her husband Howard Harriman and their two children Hilda and Rick, who were always good fun, would be there as well, and the one photo I have of these outings captures Gale in the background sitting in the car, drinking a beer, and, in the foreground, Julia from the back, bending over in her black bathing suit to pick up something from the ground—the moment the photographer, Gale's brother-in-law, had been waiting for.

Out on the Plymouth road now and approaching the State Park, my mother and I talked about the two Gales, one of which my mother and her family, who had mostly grown accustomed to him, still somewhat regretted. This was the one who lost jobs because of his drinking problem, spent money carelessly, lived with Julia in a series of run-down houses and, especially as he grew older, could become tedious and boastful and incoherent when he had taken a few drinks too many. But then there was always the other one, which it was easier, perhaps, for us as children to see and never to lose sight of: the one who always showed great interest in all that we did or said, the one who performed feats of agility and strength—holding his arms straight out from his sides to let us swing on them, jumping over a broom stick he held extended horizontally in front of him—the one who made up songs about us and sang them when we were all out in the car with him, the one who handled with great care the rabbits he kept in hutches on the hill behind his house, and his dogs, especially Lady, his beloved collie and spitz, mixed breed. He talked softly and affectionately to all animals, seeming to understand their feelings and to know their language. His great workman's hands had a gentle touch, and I can still feel his thick fingers wrapped carefully around my small hand as he pretended to lose to me in arm wrestling, just as I sensed, somehow, years later when I had my own children, that I was sometimes holding them with *his* hands, encircling them with *his* arms. As we balanced the two people we knew him to be, Mother branched off onto a secondary road, and the landscape we were passing through became, at least for me, more and more transparent until it was eclipsed by scenes from the past brought forth by our recollections.

Then she slowed the car and turned into what looked to be a long driveway, and a small house came into view among the trees, and I found myself suddenly in the present. And yes, though it seemed hard to believe, those dear people from long ago were there and waiting for us. In a rush of wonder and affection, I turned to my mother and said, "I . . ." and then discovered that I could say no more. I couldn't speak. She smiled and slowed the car and said, "I know, just go," and I was out the passenger door, my feet hitting the gravel before she had come to a full stop, and running—across the grass and up the front steps, where I hastily knocked on the door too loudly, but couldn't wait for them to answer. They had evidently heard the car approach but were hardly out of their chairs when I burst in and went for them. By the time Mother caught up, I had just released Julia and was getting as good a bear hug from Gale as I was giving. I think I managed, at first, only to say, "I am *so glad* to see you," or "I have not seen you in *such a long time!*"—something no doubt inadequate for the heart's truth, as words often are. We stayed a while and had some coffee and muffins and talked. We spoke of Abe, who had finished college and enlisted in the Navy. But what other news and information we exchanged is now beyond recall and even then was incidental to what I was looking for: the simple fact of their being there and being fully and completely themselves, older perhaps, but otherwise unchanged. As though they and not I had come back from somewhere a long way off, it was their faces and voices, their presence that counted most. And their eyes told me that this was for all time.

That brief trip from Woodstock to Bridgewater and from Bridgewater to Plymouth was a necessary journey back through the years, as I think my mother knew it would be. In asking me to accompany her, she was enabling me to discover how much we all still belonged to each other and to honor and renew something I scarcely understood when we set out from home. It gave me my first intimation of the way those people, whose mortality I had not yet allowed myself to consider, would be with me throughout their lifetimes, and even beyond. For although that brief reunion took place half a century ago and they have all passed on, time does not diminish them. "How they do live on," Frederick Buechner remarks, "those giants of our childhood, and how well they manage to take even their own death in stride because although death can put an end to them right enough, it can never put an end to our relationship with them." Age shows us their fixed places; their faces appear more often and more clearly with the passing years as though they have come back to participate in the new ways we understand them, and when we whisper their names into the darkness at the edge of sleep, we find them here, right here beside us.

Eating Soap

I was not one of those children who were punished for cursing by being forced to eat soap. In fact, I never knew how bad soap tasted until I was in my 60s and tried it myself, more or less voluntarily. I had taken the train from New Haven, Connecticut to New York City to attend an early evening poetry reading at the Lillian Vernon House on West 10th Street and had arrived at my destination at least an hour ahead of time. I was so early, in fact, that the people in charge were just connecting the sound system and testing it and setting out programs, and there was only one person sitting in the chairs extending back from the podium in the two adjoining rooms—an attractive young lady with dark hair and a pleasant looking face. I chose a seat at the end of the row in which she was sitting and put my book bag and jacket down on two chairs next to mine to save them for my son, Jonathan, and his girlfriend Ilana, who would be joining me, and sat down. Then my stomach reminded me that I had eaten next to nothing for lunch, and that I was very thirsty. Perplexed about how I could slip out in search of food and drink and still manage to keep my three seats, I nerved myself to ask the young lady if she would mind watching my things while I went out for a few moments. She smiled and answered, "Not at all" and told me not to hurry.

So I walked over to Sixth Avenue to look for a newsstand where I might find some Nabs, as they used to be called in my childhood—those packaged peanut butter crackers to which I have had a lifetime's addiction—or a grocery store that might carry wrapped sandwiches. After scouring a couple of blocks north and south without success, I decided that I shouldn't risk taxing the patience of the young lady, and I headed back, more or less resigned to going hungry and thirsty. Then, near the corner of Sixth Avenue and 10th Street, I was accosted by two women handing out small wrapped objects, one of which I gladly accepted without hearing anything of their sales pitch because of the noise of the city all around me. Assuming I had just been given food samples, I hastily unwrapped what appeared to be white chocolate or marzipan, threw the wrapper into a waste can, took a sizable bite and began chewing (I am, in spite of my parents' efforts for years to change me, not a slow eater and have always had a tendency to bolt my food, especially when feeling half-famished). Suddenly, I realized that I had a mouthful of something that was not food at all, and a burning sensation in my throat brought the realization that I had swallowed some of whatever it was. Turning onto 10th Street, I spit the mouthful of what by that time I suspected might be some kind of soap into the gutter and wiped my lips off with my handkerchief and began hawking. I very much needed a drink of water and something to help take the dreadful taste away, and figured that my best bet would be to find the men's room when I got back into the Lillian Vernon House.

The first thing I did when I re-entered the room and saw the young lady sitting and reading and watching over my things was to tell her, in some consternation, what I thought I had just done, and ask her to stay put for a short while longer. She looked at me in some amazement and alarm and then told me to go ahead, assuring me that she'd be right there when I returned. One of the officials directed me up the stairs and to the left, and I wasted no time getting there. On the second floor was a classroom with a seminar in session right across the hall from the men's room, and the students were momentarily distracted, I noticed, by my coughing as I opened the door and hastily entered. Once in there, I scooped water into my hands from the tap and slurped it up, rinsing my mouth and trying to put out the burning in my throat. I coughed and hawked and gagged and spit and slurped more water, realizing as I was doing so that I was making a lot of noise. When I finally dried my hands and face and opened the door and stepped into the hall, the classroom was quiet, and the eyes of all the students were directed my way at the old guy whom they had just heard choking and, for all they knew, violently expiring. I hastily slid out of sight and down the stairs with the taste of soap still in my throat. "Are you all right?" the girl asked, looking up at me with her big brown eyes. "Well, better, I guess, but I can't seem to get rid of that awful taste." "How did you do it?" she queried, and I told her my absurd story. Though I could tell she saw the humor in it, she was still, bless her heart, more concerned than amused. And she had an idea. While I was gone, the people in charge of the reading had set up a table of refreshments—cheese and crackers, strawberries, wine, and bottles of cold beer. It seemed to her that a beer and some food might be more effective than water in taking the soap taste out of my throat. With that suggestion, I realized that, although I didn't yet even know her name, I was beginning to find this strange young lady very appealing, indeed. I told her that I thought the refreshments were supposed to be consumed after the reading and not before, and for that reason I was reluctant to chance it by being the first one up to the table. But she wasn't; "I'll go and try it," she said, and before I could say anything, she was out of her seat. She walked up to the table and filled a paper plate with strawberries and cheese and opened a beer and then rejoined me. Her success prompted me to do the same, and very shortly we were clinking our bottles in way of introduction. Strongly suspecting that I might be in the presence of an angel, I studied her carefully. Her name, she said, was Veronica, and she and her husband, a Ph.D. student in musical composition at Columbia, were Canadian. As we were talking and getting to know each other, Jonathan and Ilana arrived. Hearing about the foolish thing I had done, Jonathan in some alarm, immediately wanted to know where I had been handed the small package and went out to Sixth Avenue to try to check on exactly what it was that I had ingested. He soon returned with a wrapped cake of soap, which I could identify, and we studied the information on the packaging to be sure I'd not swallowed poison.

By this time, the rooms were pretty much filled with people, and the reading by Scottish poet Don Paterson began.

After it was over, I suggested that we all adjourn to the White Horse Tavern on Hudson and 12th, an old haunt of mine from the mid 60s, for more beer and a bite to eat. So off we went, Ilana and Veronica walking together behind Jonathan and me and talking about what they had in common, which was music. Veronica and her husband had made some CDs of their own compositions and had some gigs in New York; Ilana was a keyboard player and vocalist for a Celtic fusion band that performed up and down the east coast. It was a pleasant time at the White Horse; we found a quiet table and talked about music and poetry, and I discovered that Veronica was a poet as well as a composer. That night, when we left and went our separate ways at the Eighth Avenue subway, we exchanged email addresses and phone numbers, and a few weeks later she and I and my daughter and three other friends managed to get together once again for another poetry reading in the Village. By that time I had read and greatly enjoyed the poems she had sent me and had gone on YouTube to see her in performance and sample her interesting and unusual new age musical compositions. But this was, as it turned out, the last time I saw her. Outside a bar in the West Village, where we went briefly after the reading, we hugged goodbye. I was regretting that I had a train to catch from Grand Central and wishing I could stay longer and make a night of it with the others. We kept up emails for a time, and then I stopped hearing from her, though Ilana stayed in touch with her for a few months on Facebook. Evidently, when her husband finished his degree, they moved back to Canada, where they are continuing to pursue their musical careers. I was a little disappointed when my emails began to go unanswered, but then, I reasoned, she was only in her 20s and had years and adventures ahead of her which would no doubt prove more memorable than our interlude. At least what seemed to me to be the vast size of her future might very well encourage her to think so.

As I have become older, I have developed a tendency to talk to strangers much more readily than I did when I was young. It is something that still seems a little unnatural to my children—as it would have to me at their age—and, I suppose, to those of their generation wholly absorbed in public by their smart phones and other electronic devices. Admittedly, it takes a little nerve, initially, to utter those first words which may be construed as a violation of privacy rather than a friendly overture. But what, after all, is there to lose? The impulse is not, for me at least, the stereotypical need to confess something to someone I will never see again, for there were no such people in the small Vermont town where I was born and raised, and so I grew up thinking that whoever was around would be there for the long haul. And it mostly goes against something in my nature to assume that I will not cross paths with someone, stranger or not, ever again, or that I will forget them. Because the world is so much larger and more variously populated than I grew up thinking it was, the intersection at any given moment of my life with the lives of the particular people I find myself next to (why them and not someone else?) has always seemed to me to be not a coincidence but rather the work of cosmic design. Rabbi Abraham Heschel tells us, "The portion of space my body occupies is taken up by myself in exclusion of anyone else. Yet no one possesses time. There is no moment which I possess exclusively. This very moment belongs to all living men as it belongs to me. Through my ownership of space, I am rival to all other beings, through my living in time, I am a contemporary of all beings." Perhaps we could classify homo sapiens as either space people, with their inviolable self-possession, or time people, with their natural affinity to any traveler on this journey taking us all to the same place regardless of our separate destinations. I confess to being the latter. Whatever the ethical possibilities of that assumption may be, at least it tends to make me more than usually attentive to the strangers I fall in with. Though the chances are, realistically speaking, very small that I will ever come across Veronica again, what is imprinted on my memory is precisely the quality of her attention to someone she knew nothing about, the instinctive earnestness and the look of sympathy and human concern in her eyes when she might, understandably, have hastened to escape from the lunatic fringe of the strange man bending over her in some distress to tell her in confidence that only moments ago he might have eaten some soap.

Acknowledgments

I wish here to thank a number of people who read parts of this book as it was being rewritten, and gave me their approval and encouragement: Ron Briggs, Howard Coffin, Dave Doubleday, Susan Elderkin, Jim Fish, Chuck Gundersen, Frank Harvey, Tilde Hungerford, Tom Hungerford, Jane Martin, and Abe Merriam. Special thanks to Liz Van Hoose for her time and her careful reading and editorial suggestions, and to Matt Wood for his interest, his generosity and his artistic skills in designing the book cover; to Jireh Billings and Adrianne Flower of F. H. Gillingham & Sons (where I still sense the presence of my Grandfather Coffin) for supplying me with a number of old photographs; to Matt Powers, Jennie Shurtleff, and Becky Talcott of the Woodstock History Center for their interest in my work and their ongoing support.

I thank my late friend Jack Moore for the hours we spent reminiscing about old Woodstock and for the place he continues to occupy in my life.

I am very grateful to Chris Forhan, the poet and memoirist who read and carefully critiqued the long first draft of "Patrimony" and offered suggestions and encouragement that led to significant revisions. His memoir, *My Father Before Me,* was also an inspiration to me.

I am especially grateful to my wife, Maria, for her remarkable memory, her many helpful recollections of my family, and her understanding and support as these pieces were being written and assembled.

And I am most deeply indebted to my old friend and editor, the novelist and publisher Bruce Hartman. To him I owe the inspiration for the paperback edition of *The Long Light of Those Days,* which rekindled interest in that book. And without his generosity, his continuing interest and encouragement and editorial acumen, this second book quite likely never would have appeared.

About the Author

Bruce Coffin is the author of *The Long Light of Those Days,* which since its first publication in 2005 has become a New England classic. He was raised in Woodstock, Vermont, and enjoyed a long career as a teacher in independent schools in England and America. For many years, until his recent retirement, he was a member of the English department at Westover School in Middlebury, Connecticut. He is married with two grown children, and divides his time between Connecticut and Vermont.

Made in the USA
Middletown, DE
25 May 2020

95831203R00156